WARRIOR *for* CHRIST

Overcoming Cancer By Faith

Peter Schuler

WARRIOR FOR CHRIST: OVERCOMING CANCER BY FAITH
by Peter Schuler

ISBNs: 978-1-953625-08-3 Trade Paperback | 978-1-953625-09-0 Ebook

Copyright 2021 Peter Schuler

Published by Intelligent Design Press. All rights reserved. No portion of this work may be reproduced in any form, with the limited exception of brief quotations in editorial reviews, without express written permission from the publisher. For permissions, or for bulk orders of church, classroom, or library copies, contact info@intelligentdesign.press.

Photographs by Peter Schuler.

Unless otherwise noted, all scripture quotations are from the Revised Standard Version of the Bible, Copyright © 1946, 1952, 1971 National Council of the Churches of Christ in the United States of America. Used by permission. All rights reserved worldwide.

Intelligent Design Press
An imprint of Kelley Creative
Spokane, Washington, USA

Warrior for Christ
Overcoming Cancer By Faith

by Peter Schuler

INTELLIGENT DESIGN PRESS

To All Brave Cancer Warriors

"For whatever is born of God overcomes the world; and this is the victory that overcomes the world, our faith."
1 John 5:4

"In the world you will have tribulation; but be of good cheer, I have overcome the world."
John 16:33

Contents

Introduction — 1

1. The Call of God — 7
2. Healing of a Crippling Injury — 10
3. Healing of a Seven-Year Terminal Illness — 12
4. Spiritual Warfare — 21
5. Persecution — 36
6. Overcoming Evil with Good — 46
7. Call of Jesus into Ministry — 48
8. "Terminal" Cancer — 64
9. Overcoming Cancer by the Resurrection — 80
10. A New Ministry — 86
11. Overcoming Pain — 89
12. Why Do We Have to Suffer? — 93
13. Supporting Those Who Are Suffering — 105
14. Praising God in the Storm — 111
15. Victory in Jesus! — 115

Introduction

At the time of this writing, I am in a battle between life and death with Stage Four incurable cancer which resulted in the substantial deterioration of my back. I have been in extreme pain for nearly two years from the eleven compression fractures of my vertebrae: L1, L2, L3, L4, and L5; T12, T11, T10, T8, T4, and T3. Jesus does a miracle in my life every day and gives me supernatural strength to walk with chronic pain. The army of the Lord—5,200 believers from all over the world—are praying for my healing. The Lord gave me a vision of healing over a year ago, and I live by faith as I wait for His perfect time to fulfill His promise. The devil and his armies of darkness seek to kill and destroy me, but they have already lost. Jesus is the King of Kings and Lord of Lords and all power in heaven and earth has been given to Him. Some people who have heard portions of my testimony tell me that I must be a courageous man of great faith. I always reply, "I am a weak man with a little faith in a great God." The power is not in our faith, but in the Lord who does the impossible. Jesus has carried me through all of these difficult trials and tribulations, and all glory and honor and praise go to Him. In the midst of severe pain, I will lift my hands to my Father, the Creator of all things, and give Him thanks. I will walk by faith and I will love Jesus to my last breath—and then throughout eternity. I will praise and worship my Lord and King.

It has been a blessing to walk with the amazing and glorious Creator for forty-eight years on many glorious mountain tops and through many valleys of suffering. God called me forty-four years ago, and I experienced the glory of His presence as I was surrounded by hundreds of angels in ascending balconies. The Lord told me to take off my shoes because I was standing on holy ground. Since that day, I have devoted my life to seeking the Lord with all my heart and to please Him as a good and faithful servant. I look forward to hearing Jesus say to me at the end, "Well done, good and faithful servant, you have been faithful over a little, I set you over much; enter into the joy of your master" (Matthew 25:2). I have always been amazed that our lives could please God, the Eternal Creator of all things. I pray that I will never compromise or become lukewarm. The Lord has healed me of a crippling injury and a terminal seven-year illness. The Father has carried me through many years of persecution and spiritual warfare, and He taught me how to overcome evil with good. Jesus called me into a glorious twenty-five-year ministry to the homeless and to those in prisons and nursing homes. I have learned to trust God through the storms and walk by faith above the circumstances of my life. Faith connects us to the one who has all power and authority. In Mark, a woman with an incurable flow of blood, who had suffered for twelve years under many physicians, reached out by faith and touched the Author of Life. Instantly, the power of God flowed into her and healed her (Mark 5:25-33). I reach out to the Lord every day and the resurrection power of Christ raises me up above the pain, sickness, fatigue, loneliness, and despair of cancer. Amen! Hallelujah!

Why write a book on faith, sickness, and suffering? Suffering and pain have been the reality for those who live in this world since the fall of man in the garden. The Lord revealed to me years ago that I have the gift of faith and that I have been called to suffer for Christ. The Lord recently called me to write a book to inspire others to seek the Lord in the midst of suffering, and to rise up by faith in the resurrection power of Christ. In some ways, it has been difficult to write about the suffering that I have endured, but it also has been a healing process for me. It is time for the hidden things that have occurred on this journey to come into the light. "For there is nothing hid, except to be made manifest; nor is anything secret, except to come to light" (Mark 4:22). I have shared what the Holy Spirit has instructed to reveal—the remainder will come to light when Jesus returns and judges all things. Come, Lord Jesus, come.

There is joy and gratefulness in my heart despite the many battles I have endured in this life. God's Word teaches that the joy of the Lord is our strength (Nehemiah 8:10). Jesus has carried me through all of them and I will praise and worship Him forever! The healing of my heart has been more profound than my physical healing. The Lord has answered my prayers and washed away all the anger, bitterness, and resentment of the past. I am very thankful that the Lord has chosen to reveal Himself to me. I am a sinner saved by grace and I am eternally grateful for all His blessings. About twenty years ago I saw a vision of Jesus after He was raised from the dead. The Lord wanted me to see that Jesus carried no bitterness or anger from the rejection of His people, the unjust crucifixion, and the suffering that He endured. He was pure and holy, and clothed in pure white garments. I asked Jesus to heal my heart from all the cruelty and suffering that I had experienced. He has been faithful to purify my heart and mind, as I forgave all who had harmed me. In the book of Daniel, Shadrach, Meshach, and Abednego came out of the fiery furnace without the smell of smoke—they carried none of the effects of their suffering (Daniel 3:26-27). My prayer is that Jesus will take me through the trials of this life without any smell of smoke from the past, and that He will remove any hardness in my heart and give me the heart of Jesus.

It is my prayer that this book will inspire others to rise up by faith and walk with Jesus to overcome the storms in their lives! Amen! Hallelujah!

Jesus promised me about three years ago:

"You will rise, Peter,

You will rise above them all."

The Lord spoke this to me on the night He called me to write this book:

"You will be one who rises up, Peter."

Peter Schuler

Warrior for Christ | Introduction

Praise God, Hallelujah! God will accomplish His plan and will for my life. He will fulfill His purpose for me (Psalms 138:8). The Lord will raise me up from all the evil, pain, and suffering and I will spend eternity in His glorious presence!

1 | The Call of God

In my first book, *In Pursuit of God: A Love Story*, the Lord called me to share all the goodness that He has shown me as I walked with Him for forty-six years. The Lord has blessed me, and I am very thankful for the years that I have walked in fellowship with Him in His glorious presence. It has been a difficult path, but my journey to know God has been glorious. The Lord has shown me visions, dreams and often speaks to me through the Holy Spirit. I am in love with Jesus and He loves me. I treasure my relationship with the Father above all else. I often fall short when I take my eyes off of Him and onto myself or things in this world. The Lord is always gracious and forgives me. I have sought to be like Enoch, who walked with God so closely that one day he entered into heaven (Genesis 5:21-

24). We are called to stay in fellowship with God every day—whether at work or at play, while shopping, driving, or at home.

By the grace of God, I started following Jesus when I was young. Several years later, I moved to the mountains and I have many wonderful memories of skiing in fellowship with the Father. He created the mountains, the sun and the snow, and gave me the ability to ski. My Creator enjoyed spending time with me as I skied with all my might. They were days of pure joy when I lifted my hands to God in praise. The Lord raised me up into His presence in heavenly places, above the world around me. I often spent time with the Father in glorious solitude as I cross-country skied across pure white snow. I was in perfect peace because my mind was set on Him (Isaiah 26:3). Truly, God is good! The Lord has graciously showed me the beauty of His creation as I traveled to Canada and across Europe on my motorcycle.

I walked with God in Switzerland as He gave me a vision of the new heaven and earth. The Father touched me and everything around me began to glow with His glory. The Lord showed me that the Church will live in perfect harmony with Him and with His creation in the new earth. I hiked with the Father on mountain trails in Idaho, often in the presence of His wonderful creatures. I loved His creation because it is an expression of Him. I love Him because He is my heavenly Father. I explored the Lord's creation on foot, bicycle, and motorcycle as I viewed the glorious splendor of His beauty. These experiences were a glimpse of the inheritance which He has prepared for His beloved children. Christ will soon reign with His Church on a new earth that will be more glorious than we can even imagine. I worshiped God with my guitar beside clear mountain lakes, in quiet meadows, and on mountain tops. I have spent many hours with the Father photographing His amazing creation. I often felt that the Lord was putting on a show just for me, and I was in awe of His beauty. I share some of these photographs in this book so others can see God's glory and worship Him.

God called me forty-four years ago as I was driving to Church on a Wednesday night. Suddenly, I was in the *shekinah* Glory of God. I looked up and I saw hundreds of angels looking down in ascending circular balconies that reached up to heaven. I was told to take off my shoes because I was standing on holy ground. God spoke three things to me: "Thou are my chosen one," "Thou shalt bless all the nations," and "I am God." I was filled with joy because of the awesome splendor of God's presence, and I never wanted to leave. He crippled my hands and then healed them as a sign that He was going to take away my life and then give it back again. This word was fulfilled four years later in 1981 when I went through a seven-year nearly terminal illness. I saw Paul in a spiritual body and the Father told me that like Paul I had been called to suffer. The Lord chose this path of suffering for me, and I was obedient to the will and plan of God. I was filled with great joy as I drove to the Church service. I was told by other members of the Church that I appeared to be glowing with God's glory. The first song that we sang began with these words: "I saw the Lord and He was high and lifted up and His train filled the Temple."

2 | Healing of a Crippling Injury

Jesus has led me through many difficult trials, and He has always given me the power to lay down my life and the power to be raised up again (John 10:18). In the mid-nineties, the Lord took me through a time of testing when my hip was shattered in twelve places after an accident. The surgeon performed a six-and-a-half-hour surgery when he inserted plates and screws to repair my bone. The doctor said that there was a good chance that the bone was beyond repair and that I would never walk again. I replied to him, "God will do a miracle and heal me." I had no health insurance to pay for the large medical bills, and I received no physical therapy. In addition, my "friend" who was claiming to help me relapsed on drugs, stole my debit card, my truck and all my emergency money. I was confined to my bed for about two months, and I began to pray five to seven hours a day to my Heavenly Father. The pain was extreme and all I could do is cry out for mercy. Surely, He hears the cry of His Saints. Gradually, the pain lessened, and I was strong enough to read the Word. I started reading at the beginning of Genesis and ended at the last chapter of Revelation. The Lord lifted me up into heavenly places, and I spent the next several months in His presence. I walked by faith above the pain and the circumstances of my situation in an amazing time of revelation. I turned over my medical and financial problems to the Father and sought Him with all my heart. God was faithful to heal me completely and He miraculously took care of my medical bills and financial issues. We serve an amazing and loving Heavenly Father who is faithful to deliver us in times of need! Later, I went back to see the doctor, and he acknowledged that it was a miracle that I was walking.

3 | Healing of a Seven-Year Terminal Illness

The Lord called me to my deepest valley when I was twenty-seven years old. Four years earlier, the Father had spoken a word of Prophecy to me that He would take away my life and then give it back again. He gave me a sign by crippling my hands and then healing them. His promise of healing gave me hope as I lived on the edge of death for seven years. By grace, Jesus lifted me up and carried me through much pain and hardship. In 1981, I came home from work and my leg began to swell out to about twice its size. I went to the doctor, and he told me that I could go to the hospital, but it would be a waste of money because there was a good chance that I would be dead by the next day. I went back to see the doctor seven years later to tell him that I had survived, but I was informed that he had passed away. God decides how long we live—not doctors. The swelling spread to my other leg and then to my whole body. My liver and kidneys stopped functioning properly and I was filled with yellow jaundice. My body was swollen with fluid and my weight went from one hundred and seventy-five pounds to about five hundred pounds. The poisons which filled my body stopped most bodily functions. Food could no longer break down in my stomach, and it would rot in my digestive tract and then pass through me undigested. My stomach was so swollen that I was often afraid it would burst. I would chew the same piece of meat in my mouth for hours because I lacked enzymes in my body to break it down. I developed severe insomnia and I was able to sleep for only a couple hours a week for the next seven years. I lived at night, and I did not go outside during the day. The pain in my body was nearly unbearable and I had the strength to face only one second at a time. I was too weak to even think that the suffering would continue in the future. Jesus gave me the grace to endure the suffering. He bore the pain for me, and He carried me through those darkest of times. All glory goes to Him!

My body stopped functioning, but my spirit soared with God. My body was wasting away but my inner nature was being renewed by the Lord (2 Corinthians 4:16). During this time, the Father revealed Himself to me in an amazing way and He opened my eyes to see the spiritual realm that is usually hidden behind a veil. My body was nearly dead, but my spirit was alive with God. Like John, I was called through the door into the spiritual world that is usually hidden from our eyes (Revelation 4). The Lord allowed me to see the great spiritual battle that is occurring around us in these end times. The illness took

away my body, mind, and mental health, but my spiritual awareness was greatly intensified. I was dead in the flesh and alive in the Spirit.

As I walked in the Spirit, my body continued to waste away from the results of the sickness. I went through my savings account and lived in extreme poverty without any assistance from the government, family, or friends. I wore old clothes that I found in a dumpster behind a local thrift store. God was always there faithfully carrying me through the darkest times. Sometimes, I went a week at a time without eating. The fluid made me look overweight, but in fact I was starving from lack of food. I wandered the streets at five hundred pounds filled with poison, and people would walk to the other side of the street to avoid me. Others would laugh at my size, appearance, and smell. Some would mock and call me "Hippo Pete." No one ever stopped to help me, and I felt like more of an animal than a human being. One day, I stood starving for food outside a grocery store with eleven cents in my pocket, watching people buy fifty-pound bags of dog food. At that point, I wished that I was a dog so that someone would have compassion on me and give me some food. For the past twenty-five years, I have been called to minister to those in need and I understood what it feels like to be treated as less then human. I sought to treat them with dignity and respect because they are all loved by God.

At twenty-seven years old, the illness caused my hair to turn gray and fall out. I felt like every molecule of my body had been destroyed. I was so weak that I was unable to read even one line in a book. Gradually, I lost my ability to read and write. I was able to walk only a couple steps at a time. By God's Grace, I survived without any human assistance. I lived at night when the outside temperatures were down to twenty below zero in the winter. My only jacket was an old, medium-sized jacket that did not fit. Jesus carried me through this illness for seven years. My liver and kidneys stopped functioning, and my immune system was very weak. The poisons that filled my body began to destroy my brain cells. After several years I began to lose all memory of my past. I had two college degrees, but I no longer knew that 2 + 2 = 4. I had spent twenty-seven years learning many things that were lost in a few months. I was once a top athlete, but the illness made it difficult to walk even a couple steps. My appearance was so changed that I became unrecognizable. My friends and family deserted me and offered no assistance. The poisons were coming out of me in the form of sweat and I smelled like rotten flesh. People would avoid me because of my appearance, size, clothes, and the odor of my body. In this world I felt like a dead man walking, but by the Grace of God, I still walked with Him in the Spirit. My eyes were yellow from jaundice and I was extremely malnourished. My legs were in constant pain and frequently cramped up. I had several heart attacks from the malnutrition and lack of potassium. My memory was erased and I had forgotten who I was and what I had done in my past. I lived one day at a time in "survival mode" for seven years.

The chemicals in my body also caused me to become seriously mentally ill. I was severely depressed, and I felt that I had fallen into a deep pit. I was very angry and paranoid, and I viewed this world as a system designed to starve me to death. I developed OCD and lived by many rituals and routines. Years later, I was called to do outreach to the seriously mentally ill who lived on the street, and the Lord used these experiences to help me minister to them. I was alone and abandoned, but I still had my faith in God and His promise to heal

me. I had no medical insurance, no doctors, no friends or family support, but God was with me. I cleaved to Him. I could not save myself—only God could deliver me. Surely, the Lord is near to all those who call upon Him!

I was under intense spiritual attack from the enemy. He hated me and sought to kill me because I belonged to God. I put my life in God's hands and believed that Jesus would be faithful to carry me through this valley and heal me. In the story of Job, the enemy was permitted to take away Job's family, possessions, and health, but the Lord remained in control, and He gave the devil strict boundaries to protect Job. Job didn't understand why all this evil was happening to him, but he put his trust in God. Like Job, I had been called to suffer and be refined in the fire of affliction. The enemy was inflicting pain on me, but the Lord would not let him kill me. I believed that Jesus would rescue me from the power of the evil one and send His promised healing. In the end, like Job, my life was restored, and I was given great blessings. Thank you, Lord!

At the Father's appointed time, He sent His Spirit into my seemingly lifeless body, and I stood up on my feet. The Spirit breathed life into my "dead body" and I was raised from the grave. He miraculously sent some money to me in the mail to provide for my needs, and the promised time of healing and resurrection had finally come! My enemies were shocked to see me rise up in the Spirit, because they had believed the lies of the devil that they could kill me. The money was an inheritance from my grandfather that was scheduled to be given to me several years before, but my family refused to tell the State of Oregon how to locate me. The Lord interceded and made them disclose my location just before the money was scheduled to go back to the State. For the next several years, the Father caused the fluids to be expelled from my body at a rate of about seventy pounds a year. Gradually, He taught me how to walk again and I began to practice every day to regain my strength. I remember the day that I made it up a small one-hundred-foot hill. I was so excited—it seemed like I had climbed Mount Everest. For several years, the Father took me back through my childhood and restored to me the memories of my previous life. My Heavenly Father, who had created me, still remembered who I was (Psalm 139). Gradually, He healed my body, mind, and soul until I was a new creation in Christ. The Father did a miracle and restored my ability to do all the sports and activities that I had enjoyed before the illness. I started to ski, hike, climb mountains, cross-country ski, ride a motorcycle, and bicycle ride again. By the grace of God, I ascended 5,000 vertical feet in one day to the top of a 12,000-foot peak, which was the highest one in the area. With the Lord's help, I was able to ski, hike, and bike ride at the same level of proficiency as I did before the illness. At the beginning of this process of healing, my body was still weak and filled with fluid. Gradually, the Father gave me back my life in the mountains, and I walked with Him again in His Glorious Creation. Truly, the Lord is a God of miracles and healing.

The Father restored the memory of what I had learned in twenty years of school. I studied a GED book, and I regained my ability to read, write, and do basic math. Father chose not to restore my complete memory, but He gave me back what He wanted me to remember. Gradually, I began to talk, think, and learn again. The Lord was my doctor, physical therapist, and my psychiatrist. The Father breathed life into me and raised me from the dead. I had been crucified with Christ, and now He lives in me forever! We serve a truly amazing God!

The Lord's healing of my heart was even more amazing than my physical healing. I had developed many serious mental problems during the illness: severe depression, paranoia, schizophrenia, anger, and bitterness. I felt rejected and alone as I laid in my room of suffering. I also developed severe PTSD from the trauma of my illness. The Lord revealed to me that He wanted to heal the hurt and anger that was in my heart. He said that I had roots of bitterness growing inside me from all the cruelty and suffering that I had experienced. When a current event triggered my anger, God would then reveal to me the causes of the bitterness that had been hidden from my view. He then gave me the choice to forgive and be set free, or to hold on to the resentment and be miserable. The emotional healing took years because the roots of bitterness had accumulated for most of my life. God's light exposed the darkness, and I chose to let go and be healed. He restored my life and then called me to minister to broken and hurting people. The Father showed me that I would be able to comfort people that were suffering with the same comfort that God had comforted me with during my illness (2 Corinthians 1:3-6). Looking back, I can see God's plan and purpose in these years of suffering. This testimony is based on a chapter in my first book, *In Pursuit of God: A Love Story*.

4 | Spiritual Warfare

Spiritual warfare, demons, and the devil are difficult subjects that many want to avoid, yet the Word of God teaches that we are called to be spiritual warriors in an ongoing battle with the devil and his army of demons. If I had my own way, I would have avoided all the spiritual battles that I have endured in my life. There were times when the Lord has led me to rest in the safety of His glorious presence, but He has also called me to be a spiritual warrior. Through many battles, the Lord has molded me into a warrior for Christ, and I became strong in the Lord and in His Word to overcome the evil one (1 John 2:14). We can't hide in the crib forever—the Lord has called us to grow up and become His army to carry the light of the Gospel to the world of darkness. I have learned that the Lord is with us in every battle, and He prepares a table for us in the presence of our enemies (Psalm 23:5). Since the time of Christ, true believers have conquered the devil by the blood of the Lamb and the word of their testimony: that they loved not their lives, even unto death (Revelation 12:11). The early Church was empowered by the Holy Spirit to overcome the evil one and spread the Gospel over much of the world. We are called to rise up with the strength of the Lord and resist the devil with courage and faith. The Lord spoke to Joshua as he entered into the Promised Land to battle many enemies: "Have I not commanded you? Be strong and of good courage; be not frightened, neither be dismayed; for the Lord your God is with you wherever you go." (Joshua 1:9). In the same way today, we are called to be warriors for Christ in a spiritual battle against the powers of darkness as we are obedient to fulfill the Great Commission to spread the Gospel to a world in darkness.

The enemy often deceives our family members, friends, and fellow Christians to become our enemies: "And a man's foes will be those of his own household" (Matthew 10:16-23,36; John 15:18-25). I learned to be a spiritual warrior at a young age because I was born into a family of darkness and evil. Looking back over my life, I realize that the most difficult times were what drove me to seek God with all my heart. I was raised in evil and hate, and one of the last memories of my mother was her standing at my door with an axe, shaking with rage, stating that she created me, and she was going to kill me because I didn't go to Thanksgiving dinner (I was married and living in another state). The Lord would not let her kill me, so she went home with the axe and tried to destroy a deck that I had built. My father said that she had "flown over the cuckoo's nest." After I was disowned by my family for being a Christian, I asked God why

Thou dost keep him in perfect peace, whose mind is stayed on Thee, because he trusts in Thee. Isaiah 26:3

I didn't have a "Leave it to Beaver" family (an idyllic Hollywood version of family life). The Lord answered me that I would have been comfortable, and I would not have sought Him like I did. Truly, the Lord does work in all things for good.

As a child, the enemy would frequently attack me at night by trying to paralyze me and stop me from breathing. The Holy Spirit was with me every night and kept me alive by rescuing me just before I stopped breathing. Many nights, I was the target of witchcraft, and during the day I often felt severe fatigue and exhaustion as the evil one sought to drain the life out of me. At the time, I did not understand what was happening to me, but the Lord revealed the truth to me several years later. I became hardened by hate and cruelty, but God's love broke through into my heart and delivered me. They hated me because they hated God. I have cried out to God in the midst of trials, and He has rescued me and sheltered me in the safety of His presence from the forces of darkness. Sometimes, when I felt overwhelmed by the suffering, the Lord would speak to me, "You don't know the evil that I have protected you from." Jesus truly kept me alive during many years of intense attack from the enemy. When I started following Christ, the Lord spoke these words to me: "Therefore it is said, 'Awake, O sleeper, and arise from the dead, and Christ will give you light.'" (Ephesians 5:14). He delivered me from the dominion of darkness and transferred me to the kingdom of His beloved Son (Colossians 1:13). Thank you, Jesus!

The oppression in my childhood was so strong that I did not grow or develop until I left home at eighteen. When I entered college, I looked like I was still in junior high school, and I grew about five inches during the first year of school. In the environment of evil in my home, the spiritual darkness was draining my strength and energy. Because of this, I was hindered from doing physical activities and sports, and I was usually the last person to be picked in gym class. Later, when Jesus set me free from this oppression, I flourished as an athlete and I became a top skier, hiker, mountain climber, biker, and cross-country skier. The oppression also affected my mental capabilities, and I had C average in high school. My school counselor told me not to go to college because I would fail. This motivated me to move away from home and go to college where I obtained two degrees and went to graduate school. My mother's hate for me intensified when I became a Spirit-filled, born again Christian. When I visited home, she yelled at me that I had "floated in and floated out" in the Spirit. She hated God, the Holy Spirit, and me. In my childhood, I was never held, touched, encouraged or loved—even as a baby. I heard frequent criticism, condemnation, yelling, hate, and false accusations. This hate caused me to be bound in the fear of rejection, and I became shy and withdrawn. For years, I put a wall around me to protect myself from the evil. I had difficulty letting anyone come close to me or touch me. I remember when I was about twenty-one, my father put his hand on my shoulder, and I jumped back in shock because someone had touched me. It took years for me to heal and become able to trust people. I was very afraid of speaking in front of anyone, yet later in my life, I was called to preach and lead worship services to thousands of people. For twenty-five years, the Lord anointed this broken person to lead many to Christ and minister to those who were in need.

My father was a believer, but he was not able to stand against the evil in the household. They drove him out of his own home, and for the last ten years of his life, he lived on the road with a small suitcase. The evil in the family had taken everything away from him, and they succeeded in turning him against me. They wanted all of his money, and they were afraid that he would give me an inheritance. He was not allowed to talk to me and for years he had to call me from a pay phone. He would warn me that my mother was in an angry rage, threatening to harm me. I replied that I could move to a nearby town. He advised me to move out of the county. My father died in an accident when I was young, and the Lord told me that He wanted him for reasons that I could not know at the time. The Lord allowed him to send a message back to me: "We (my wife and I) were right and he was wrong and that he was sorry." I love my father and I look forward to meeting him again in heaven.

I have learned through the years to keep most of my experiences of spiritual warfare to myself. There is often very little support for those who have been victims of witchcraft. Years ago, I attended a Church retreat where the members of the Church gave their testimonies and then received prayer and support. Many shared stories of childhood abuse, alcohol and drug addictions, and sexual immorality. The Church was very supportive of everyone's story until I gave my testimony of being a victim of witchcraft as a child. When they kicked me out of the Church, I tried to explain to them that I was a victim of witchcraft, but that I never was involved with it myself. They replied that they understood this, but they didn't want to get caught in the "crossfire." They were concerned that they would be attacked by the spiritual powers that were coming against me. The Lord has called the Church to stand together against the powers of the evil one.

The Lord has revealed to me that sickness is primarily a result of spiritual warfare. The devil is using his power to inflict pain and sickness on those who live in this world. On March 8, 2020, when the COVID virus had just begun to spread in the US, I was attacked by demons who were trying to bring the virus on me. I was experiencing sickness, pain, and night sweats. I prayed for hours, and I couldn't sleep. I began to see them in my room, and at about 4 a.m., I was directed by the Holy Spirit to pray for the blood of Jesus to cover me. I immediately saw a wall of Christ's blood that stood between me and the demons. I could see through the spaces in the drops of blood, that they were on the other side of the wall, but they could not get through to attack me. The Lord kept me safe. Praise God! That night, the Lord spoke to me concerning the pandemic that was just beginning: "Come, O sons, listen to me, I will teach you the fear of the LORD" (Psalm 34:11). The Lord is calling the world to humble themselves, repent and turn to Him to be saved. I continue to pray for those all over the world who are suffering from the COVID virus. We need to turn to Jesus who has complete authority over demons, sickness, and death (see Mark 5). Unbelief is the only force that can stop Jesus from doing a miracle in our lives (Mark 6:1-6).

The Lord has called us to stand against the evil one by putting on the whole spiritual armor of God:

> Finally, be strong in the Lord and in the strength of His might. Put on the whole armor of God, that you may be able to stand against the wiles of the devil. For we are not contending against flesh and blood, but against principalities, against powers, against the world rulers of this present darkness, against the spiritual hosts of wickedness in heavenly places. Therefore, take the whole armor of God, that you may be able to withstand the evil day, and having done all, to stand. Stand therefore, having girded your loins with truth, and having put on the breastplate of righteousness, and having shod your feet with the equipment of the gospel of peace; beside all these, taking the shield of faith, with which you can quench the flaming darts of the evil one. And take the helmet of salvation and the sword of the Spirit, which is the word of

God. Pray at all times in the Spirit, with all prayer and supplication (Ephesians 6:10-18).

The Bible teaches us that we are in a battle against the devil and his demonic principalities. The Lord has given us this armor, which is empowered by the Holy Spirit, so that we can stand against these forces of evil that seek to tempt and destroy us. The enemy has set his principalities of demons over countries, cities, Churches and even households to deceive, divide, and destroy. We use the shield of faith to protect us from the enemy's lies, accusations and deception—anything that contradicts the truth of Jesus and His Word. We are told to pray at all times, to stay strong in the Spirit to keep ourselves safe from all evil.

The Lord has given us one offensive weapon: the sword of the Spirit or the Word of God. Jesus used the Scriptures to defeat the devil in the wilderness (Luke 4:1-13). In order to be effective spiritual warriors, it is necessary to be skilled at using God's Word. For instance, when the devil is attacking us with guilt, we need to turn to scriptures like 1 John 1:9: "If we confess our sins, He is faithful and just, and will forgive our sins and cleanse us from all unrighteousness." We believe we are saved by grace through faith in the Word of God, and we do not trust in our feelings or emotions. When the enemy is attacking us with stress and worry, we can turn to Philippians 4: 6-7: "Have no anxiety about anything, but in everything by prayer and supplication with thanksgiving let your requests be made known to God. And the peace of God which passes all understanding, will keep your hearts and your minds in Christ Jesus." The Bible is telling us to pray instead of worrying, and the Lord will give us

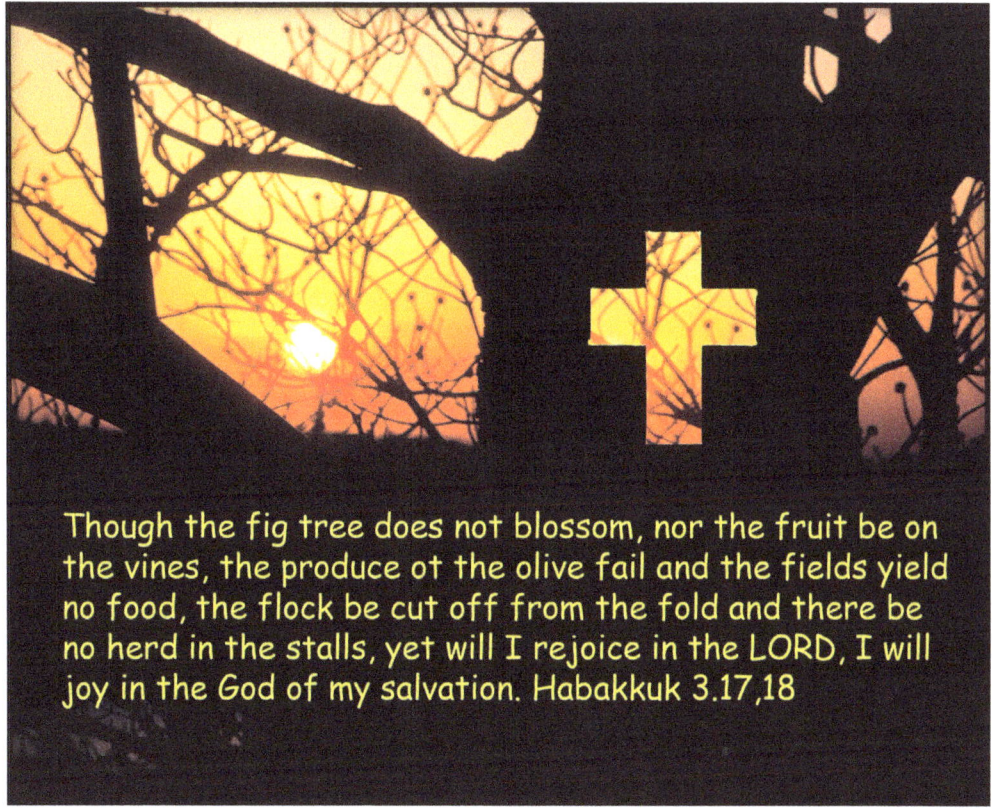

Though the fig tree does not blossom, nor the fruit be on the vines, the produce ot the olive fail and the fields yield no food, the flock be cut off from the fold and there be no herd in the stalls, yet will I rejoice in the LORD, I will joy in the God of my salvation. Habakkuk 3.17,18

a peace in our hearts and minds. We worry when we stop trusting God and try to carry the weight of our own burdens. Instead, the Word tells us to give everything to Jesus and enter into His rest. We will defeat the devil by learning to effectively stand on the power of God's Word—for the Battle is the Lord's. As warriors for Christ, we study God's Word so that we will know the correct scripture to defeat the enemy.

During my seven-year illness, I became very aware of the spiritual war that is going on behind the veil between the angels of God and the demon army of the devil. These spiritual angels are invisible to our natural eyes, and they can only be seen through spiritual eyes. When I was young, I was unable to see this spiritual realm but as my faith grew, I became more aware of God's Spirit and the spirit of darkness. The Lord revealed to me that everything that happens in the physical world is controlled and affected by spiritual wars in the heavenlies. The Word teaches that there are spiritual powers behind every world government (Daniel 10:12-21). Jesus allowed John to look beyond the veil in Revelation, where he saw God sitting on the throne with His spiritual army of angels. John saw the Lord release a series of judgments (seals, trumpets, and bowls) to deliver God's people and destroy evil. John also describes an army of Satan that rules over the world governments and the false prophet (the false church) that was deceiving this world (see Revelation chapters 4 through 19). During my illness, these forces of evil would attempt to torment me with pain, and the Lord gave me a spiritual sword to fight against them. Some mornings, my hand would be temporarily paralyzed from cleaving to the sword for many hours. The enemy had deceived several people to think that they could kill me through witchcraft—but greater is He who is in me than he who is in the world (1 John 4:4). They were amazed when God raised me up and healed me. For seven years, I saw into the spiritual realm that is usually hidden from our eyes by a veil. This world no longer seemed real, and it appeared to be like a fake Hollywood stage front designed by the devil to deceive this those who dwell on this earth. When the Lord healed me seven years later, I prayed that Jesus would take away some of my ability to see beyond the veil because I needed to be able to work and interact with the world on a normal basis.

As we grow in Christ and become more aware of the Spirit of God, we will also begin to see the spiritual darkness that surrounds us. I have seen many demons cast out of people by the power of the Holy

Spirit. When I first started following Christ, I attended a Charismatic Church that was so filled with the Holy Spirit, people were delivered from demons while they sat in the pews. They would fall down, foam at the mouth and roll around between the pews. I remember a woman waiting to be baptized, standing in front of the Church with man's clothing, short haircut and business suit. The demon in her did not want to go into the water and it spoke with a loud man's voice cursing God, the Church, and the pastor. For several years, I taught a women's Bible study for the homeless and after one service, the Holy Spirit led me to pray for one of the women. As I began to pray, the demon in her spoke with a loud voice, "I know who you are, you have come to torment me." There are numerous accounts in the Gospels of demons speaking to Jesus in a similar manner: "When he saw Jesus, he cried out and fell down before him, and said with a loud voice, 'What have you to do with me, Jesus, Son of the Most High God? I beseech you, do not torment me'" (Luke 8:28). The demons are still present on this earth today as they were in the time of Christ, but they have learned to hide themselves in this sophisticated society. We need to be careful of "deliverance" ministries, because they can sometimes do more harm than good if they are not conducted according to the Word of God and the Holy Spirit. I have a friend who attended one of these Churches and picked up demonic "hitchhikers" during the service. In Acts, some false exorcists were trying to cast out demons and ended up demon possessed: "The evil spirit answered them, 'Jesus I know, and Paul I know, but who are you?'" (Acts 19:13-20). Jesus has given His true disciples authority over the enemy: "Behold, I have given you authority to tread upon serpents and scorpions, and over all the power of the enemy, and nothing shall hurt you" (Luke

10:19). On another occasion, I attended a spiritual revival meeting where we worshiped God for two and a half hours. The Holy Spirit was so strong in the auditorium that many people were being healed, and I saw a vision of Jesus sitting on a White Throne. This all happened before the famous speaker went up on the stage—it was all the work of God and not of man. We had invited the Holy Spirit to come as we worshiped for two and a half hours, and the demons were driven out of the building. As I walked out of the auditorium, I saw a wall of demons about ten feet outside the building—they were unable to come any closer because of the power of the Holy Spirit. I put on my armor and walked back into the world, which remained under the power of the evil one.

It is essential that we test every spirit to see if it is of God (1 John 4:4). The enemy attempts to deceive us with false teaching and counterfeit signs and wonders. The enemy can imitate almost anything that God does on this earth. Satan disguises himself as an angel of light, and his followers disguise themselves and servants of righteousness (2 Corinthians 11:12-15). God anoints apostles, prophets, evangelists, pastors, and teachers to accomplish His work in this world. Satan sends out false ministers to do his work of deceiving unbelievers and even believers. The Holy Spirit gives various gifts to the Church, and Satan sends his followers to perform counterfeit signs and wonders to lead astray, if possible, even the elect (Matthew 24:24). Jesus said to the religious leaders of Christ's time who were disguised as righteous and holy men, "You are of your father the devil, and your will is to do your father's desires" (John 8:44). God allows false prophets in this world to test our hearts, to see whether we truly love and obey Him (Deuteronomy 13:1-5). We show our devotion to Christ by refusing to submit to false Christs, gospels and spirits. We must test everything by the Word of God and the Holy Spirit.

There are many "doorways" that can put us under the power of the evil one. We are protected by the Holy Spirit and the armor of God when we walk in the ways of God, but when we walk in the ways of sin and evil, we give opportunities for the enemy to control and deceive us. For example, drug use can open a door into the demonic realm. The word for drugs in the Greek, the original language of the New Testament, is *pharmakia*. It can be translated as drugs or witchcraft. The desire for power, fame, and riches can put us under the power of the evil one. Some follow the teaching of the power of positive thinking and use their mental or psychic powers to obtain what they desire in this life. Many seek more power, and they become involved with demons to obtain the things of this world. In the Church, this is called the "word faith movement." The devil offers the power, glory, success, and riches of this world to those who bow down and worship him (Luke 4:5-6). The devil is asking: "What do you want in exchange for your soul: success, power, drugs, sex, fame, mansion, fancy cars, wealth?" The whole world lies under the power of the evil one, and many people unknowingly sell their souls to the devil for the things of this world. Power becomes an addiction, and these people continue to go deeper into the ways of Satan to obtain their desired goals. I once worked for a construction contractor who revealed to me that he used witchcraft to cause a plane of a man who owed him money to crash. They begin to play God, and use their demonic power to judge, condemn, and punish those that they hate. James teaches, "This wisdom is not such as comes down from above, but is earthly, unspiritual, devilish. For where jealousy and selfish ambition exist, there will be disorder and every evil work" (James 3:15-16). Jesus warned us that if they called Him Beelzebul (a devil), they will also malign the Church (Matthew 10:25). Satan deceives his own followers, and many think they are doing God's work by persecuting God's people. The religious leaders of Christ's time thought they were obeying God when they killed Jesus. Saul was deceived by the enemy to persecute Christians until Jesus revealed the truth to him on the road to Damascus. In a similar way, there were some people who believed that they were doing God's work by devoting their lives to trying to kill me through witchcraft.

The tragic story of King Saul's fall away from God and into the power of the enemy is a warning to us today. In 1 Samuel, the Bible reveals to us how Saul started out by loving David greatly (verse 16:18), then became jealous (verses 18: 6-9) and was eventually controlled by an evil spirit to attempt to kill David (verses 18:10-15). Inspired by evil, Saul became David's enemy for thirteen years until his death. Saul was originally anointed by the Holy Spirit and became King over Israel, but he soon chose to disobey God, and a tormenting spirit overtook him. Rebellion is the sin of witchcraft (1 Samuel 15:23). He continued to walk in the ways of evil and became demon possessed. He no longer was able to communicate with God, and at the end of his life, he consulted a witch and committed suicide. The Bible teaches that anger, bitterness, unforgiveness, stealing, and evil talk grieves the Holy Spirit and allows the devil to gain a foothold over our lives (Ephesians 4:26-32). The Scriptures teach us to "Submit yourselves therefore to God. Resist the devil and he will flee from you" (James 4:7). Effective spiritual warfare begins with submitting to God, surrender, obedience, and confessing our sin. We

must first eliminate any doorways for the devil to attack us, and then we will be able to effectively resist him. Jesus has called us to go out into this world with His authority and the anointing of the Holy Spirit to battle for the souls lost in darkness.

5 |
Persecution

I have frequently experienced persecution and rejection from family, friends and fellow Christians. When I became discouraged, I would go up to the mountains to ask Him whether He was angry with me like the people that were persecuting me. He would always answer, "No Peter, I am pleased with your heart." He would then give me the strength to go back down to the valley and face more opposition. The Bible warns that persecution will be experienced by all those who truly follow Christ: "Indeed all who desire to live a godly life in Christ Jesus will be persecuted" (2 Timothy 3:12). The devil has no reason to attack lukewarm, worldly Christians. If the enemy attended a lukewarm Church, he would probably say, "Amen, keep up the good work." Jesus warns, "If the world hates you, know that it has hated me before it hated you. If you were of the world, the world would love its own; but because you are not of the world, but I chose you out of the world, therefore the world hates you" (John 15:18-19). God's Word is clear that we will be hated by all for the name of Christ (Matthew 10:22). I have been hated, excluded, and cast out by many who called themselves Christians, but by faith I continue to follow Christ. The Bible warns, "Woe to you, when men speak well of you, for so their fathers did to the false prophets" (Luke 6:26). God's Word teaches, "Blessed are you when men hate you, and when they exclude you and revile you, and cast your name as evil, on account of the Son of man! Rejoice in that day and leap for joy, for behold, your reward is great in heaven; for so their fathers did to the prophets" (Luke 6:22-23). I was recently called a Satanist on the Internet by someone who disagreed with my Biblical interpretation. I replied by thanking him for blessing me because everyone who is persecuted is blessed by God. We are told to bless those who persecute us and forgive all who have mistreated. Jesus said on the Cross, "Father forgive them for they know not what they do" (Luke 23:34). We must forgive, let go of the past, and not carry bitterness and anger with us as we serve Christ.

I have been persecuted and removed from several Churches for living and speaking the truth. Years ago, I attended a "charismatic" Church that was considered by many to be the best one in the area where I lived. When I entered the Church and joined in with the worship service, the Holy Spirit spoke to me, "They do not know who they are singing to." When they started praying, the Spirit said to me, "They do not know who they are praying to." When the pastor started preaching the Word, the Spirit continued to speak to me, "They do not know who they are talking about." At first, I had a difficult time believing that this "beautiful" Church was not of God. Gradually, I began to see the false teaching and heresy. I shared with them that God had healed me from an illness several years before. The pastor and the rest of the Church followed the health, wealth, and prosperity false gospel, and they believed that anyone who is sick or has been ill was of the devil. Ironically, after I had been removed from the Church, many members of the assembly began to get chronic illnesses.

In this money gospel, God becomes more like a Santa Claus who exists to meet their every need. At one service, the pastor told everyone in the Church to write down fifteen things that they wanted, and that God had to give it to them. The pastor's list started with a Dodge Viper and his second request was to see Hell. I stood up and stated that this was not the Gospel and I cited several scriptures. Jesus revealed to me that this was a Laodicean lukewarm apostate Church as described in Revelation 3:14-22. This Church boasted that they were rich, prosperous, and needed nothing (verse 3:17). Jesus will spew (vomit) them out of His mouth (verse 3:16). When I attended the Church, I would sometimes get physically sick because the Church was making Jesus sick. The pastor of my Church had been teaching on false prophets, and I went with them to hear a famous preacher. The Holy Spirit told me throughout the service that this preacher was a false prophet. Note: it is important that we do not judge for ourselves but test everything by the Holy Spirit and the Word of God. The preacher spoke primarily about money and said that when we have money, we have peace. He made us chant, "Citation 10," which was the name of the new jet he was buying. I prayed during the service that God would not strike him dead with lightning. When

I shared my concerns with the other Church members, they replied that they saw nothing wrong with any of the false teaching.

I went with the Church on a missionary journey to Africa. We received reports that the witchdoctors were going to use their powers of evil to make us as weak as mice. During the trip I felt weak, but I soon realized that the strongest attack of the enemy would come from inside the Church. I gave my testimony at a local Church, and the pastor complained to my pastor that I had preached on healing from an illness (he had been taught the same false teaching that Christians can never get sick). The pastor of my Church forced me to appear before an inquisition-like council, where they accused me of following the devil for the past twenty years because I had been sick. I gave them multiple scriptures to show them the error of their beliefs, but they refused to listen. On the council were my two best friends who betrayed me and sided with the pastor. I warned the pastor many times that he was in danger of blaspheming the Holy Spirit because he was attributing the work of the Holy Spirit in my life to the devil (Mark 3:29-30). The Church leaders decided that I was demon possessed, and they scheduled an exorcist to come the next morning to "deliver" me from the deceiving spirit. Fortunately, she didn't show up the next morning. I was banned from preaching for the rest of the trip, and eventually I was completely removed from the Church. God made a way for me to minister in Africa after the Church banned me from preaching. I visited a village and the Holy Spirit anointed me to dance for two and a half hours with about seventy children. The children invited their parents and the local Church experienced a dramatic revival when their attendance went from about five members to well over one hundred. At that time, I remembered that the Jews had

called Jesus the devil. Sadly, the local pastor who did not believe in sickness later sent a letter to the Church in America, begging for prayer for his son who was seriously ill.

Several months after I left that Church, the pastor was caught in adultery with a member of the Church, divorced his wife, left his children, and moved to another state. During the time I was in the Church, no one would confess the truth because they were afraid of the pastor, who attacked anyone who disagreed with him. Some members would secretly come to me and confess that they knew the pastor was wrong, but they were afraid to oppose him. Jesus declared, "Whoever denies me before men, I will also deny before my Father who is in heaven" (Matthew 10:32). Jesus was testing their hearts to see whether they would stand up for Christ and the truth, or live by fear and please men. I was finally completely thrown out of the Church, and I went to a nearby lake to pray and feel sorry for myself. The Lord asked me why I wanted to be part of that ungodly Church.

I then attended a Church three miles away, and I soon realized that the pastor of the previous Church had spread his false accusations to this pastor. The pastor stood up in front of the Church and pointed at me and declared, "Whoever says that we have to suffer is of the devil." Sadly, I was told that two or three months later, he was killed in a car accident. I left this Church and went to another one nearby where the pastor said that I could sit in the service, but I was not allowed to speak to anyone. I don't think that this is what Jesus meant when He taught us to fellowship with Christians in Church.

I was called by Jesus twenty-five years ago to the inner-city to serve those in need. I became a pastor at the largest homeless ministry in the city. The Holy Spirit anointed me to teach and lead praise and worship at the discipleship program, and in jails, prisons and nursing homes. After several years, the Spirit began to reveal to me that the Church and program was full of sin. Several pastors of the Church were addicted to drugs and would often sell their cars to the drug house for crack. Many times, the members of the program would have to rescue the pastor's vehicles from the drug dealers. One Sunday, we were sitting on the steps of the Church, and we saw one of the pastor's cars drive by filled with four drug dealers. Members of the Church chased them down and recovered the vehicle. One of the houses operated by the program was recruiting residents to sell drugs for them. There was widespread drug and alcohol use, and frequent sexual immorality between the men's and women's programs. There were many thieves living at the program who stole money from me and others at the program. Some of the residents were openly practicing witchcraft. I informed the head pastor about these issues and read to him 1 Corinthians 5: 11: "I wrote to you not to associate with anyone who bears the name of a brother if he is guilty of immorality or greed, or is an idolater, reviler, drunkard or robber—not even to eat with such a one." The pastor replied that he could not apply this scripture to his ministry because he would have to close it down. By his own words, the program was unscriptural. They were perverting the grace of God into a license to continue to sin. The Bible gives us the true purpose of grace: "For the grace of God has appeared for the salvation of all men, training us to renounce irreligion and world passions, and to live sober, upright, and godly lives in this world" (Titus 2: 11-12). The assistant pastor confronted me and stated they were trying to remove me as a pastor, but that they couldn't find any "dirt" on me. I prayed for the ministry, and the Holy Spirit called me to lead a prayer and worship service. The pastor shut it down after some members of the Church complained to him that I was "trying to make them spiritual." People would often "worship" God while high on drugs and alcohol. The pastor ordered me to allow people who were under the influence of drugs to minister with me in the nursing homes. He said that it would do them some good. The word for drugs in the original Greek can be translated as "drugs" and also "witchcraft," and I refused to bring this into my ministry. They began looking for a way to drive me out of the Church.

I continued to be obedient to the call of Jesus and ministered to those in need, but I refused to take part in ungodly sin that was practiced in the Church. The Holy Spirit continued to anoint my ministry, and many people were led to the Lord. During this time, I worked part-time doing landscape maintenance, and one Saturday, a realtor asked me to clean up the house of a man who had passed away. I had maintained his yard but had never been inside his house because he lived as a recluse like Howard Hughes. The man had died in his home, and his body had rotted through the carpet. The smell in the house was horrible, and my dust mask was ineffective. In addition, the house had not been cleaned for nine years. There was a layer of dust and dirt over one-inch-thick on every surface throughout the house. The dogs had urinated on every piece of furniture during those nine years, so much so that we had to pry them off of the rug. The Lord revealed to me that the Church smelled this bad to Him. Jesus saw the hypocrisy, drugs, drinking, sexual perversion, and all of the ungodliness that was occurring in this supposedly "Christian" ministry. I decided that I could not be involved with a Church that was this displeasing to Jesus, and I resigned as pastor on Monday morning. The pastor was very angry with me and never spoke to me again. I thank God that He had warned to get out of "Sodom and Gomorrah" before His judgment came upon them. I continued to serve Christ and help those in need for eighteen more years, but I was no longer unequally yoked to a lukewarm Church that was so displeasing to Christ.

Jesus has called the Church to love one another, but some Christians use their tongues to tear down instead of build up others. We need to be careful with our mouths because Christians are sometimes unwittingly used by the devil to persecute other members of the body. Satan is often called the accuser of the brethren, and he will use any tongue that is available to attack believers. The Lord told me

GOD, the Lord,
is my strength;
he makes my feet
like hinds' feet,
He makes me tread
upon my high places.
Hab. 3.19

several years ago that many of the words that have been spoken to me in my life were the words of Satan. Satan even deceived the apostle Peter to rebuke Jesus when after the Lord spoke of his upcoming crucifixion: "But he turned and said to Peter, 'Get behind me, Satan! You are a hindrance to me; for you are not on the side of God, but of men'" (Matthew 16:21-23). We have the power of death and life in our tongues, and we are called to speak words of life, encouragement, and grace to build up others in the faith (Proverbs 17:21). Satan the accuser often deceives the body of Christ to do his work by attacking each other. Jesus warns that a kingdom divided against itself cannot stand. Unfortunately, the Church today is divided by man-made opinions and religious and cultural traditions that do not come from God. We are one in the Spirit and divided in the flesh. Paul writes that our knowledge is imperfect and that we Christ through a mirror darkened by sin, the flesh, religion and our culture (1 Corinthians 13:9-12). The Bible reminds us that God has called us to love one another, instead of defending our own opinions and arguing with others.

I have spent many years crying out to God in the midst of persecution from family, friends, and fellow Christians. I prayed that God would protect me from my enemies and take me to a place where there was no rejection for me. I long to dwell in the safety of God's presence and far from the false accusations, condemnation, judgment, jealousy, and hate. I look forward to heaven, where people will love one another and see each other through God's eyes and not judge by appearances.

6 |
Overcoming Evil with Good

The Bible teaches, "Do not be overcome by evil, but overcome evil with good" (Romans 12:21). We live in a world that is increasingly filled with anger and hate, and devoid of love: "And because wickedness is multiplied, most men's love will grow cold" (Matthew 24:12). How do we keep ourselves from being affected by evil while we live in this world of darkness? We overcome the world by walking in the supernatural Agape love of Jesus as He taught in Luke 6:27-38. For me, this is one of the most radical sections of the Bible—especially when we try to live it out. We overcome hate by responding with good and not allowing it to harden our hearts. We overcome evil by loving our enemies, blessing those who curse us, and turning our other cheek when someone strikes us. We give to those who beg and do not seek to recover what is stolen from us. Jesus teaches us that we love others by doing for them what we want them to do for us. Jesus summarizes this passage in verses 35 and 36: "But love your enemies, and do good, and lend, expecting nothing in return, and your reward will be great, and you will be sons of the Most High, for he is kind to the ungrateful and the selfish. Be merciful even as your Father is merciful." The Church could change the world if they truly followed the teachings of Jesus. When we stand in the strength of the Lord, with the whole armor of God and our hearts filled with the love of Christ, then the living water of love will flow out of our hearts to a world trapped under the power of evil (John 7:38-39). The Bible tells us that we are to be *in* the world and not *of* it, meaning that we belong to Christ and we are called to follow His ways and not the ways of the world (John 17:11-14; Romans 12:2). The Bible instructs us to conduct ourselves in holiness in this world as we shine our lights into the darkness that surrounds us. Paul writes that we should never repay evil for evil or seek to avenge ourselves because the Lord is the Judge and avenger of all wrongs (Romans 12:14-21). We follow Jesus, who was a friend of sinners, and yet maintained personal holiness and perfect obedience to the Father. We overcome evil by walking in Christ's love in the power of the Holy Spirit.

7 |
Call of Jesus into Ministry

Jesus called me into full time ministry twenty-five years ago and asked me to leave behind my business and home and give away my money. I had walked with Him for many years in the mountains, and I planned to stay there for the rest of my life. I loved the time that I had spent with the Father in His Glorious Creation, but I also knew that I must be obedient to Christ's call on my life. Like Paul, I wanted to finish the race, be a wise and faithful servant, and please Jesus with my life. Jesus still calls us today to leave everything in this life behind and follow Him (Mark 10:28-30). The disciples obeyed Jesus, and He used them in a mighty way to change the world and save many souls. Many others through the ages have heard the same call. Paul's heart was filled with passion to follow Christ: "But I do not account my life of any value nor as precious to myself, if only I may accomplish my course and this ministry which I received from the Lord Jesus, to testify to the gospel of the grace of God" (Acts 20:24). Unfortunately, there are many who chose not to follow Christ, like the rich young ruler who loved his money more than he loved Jesus (Mark 10:17-22). The Word of God is still true today: "If any man would come after me, let him deny himself and take up his cross and follow me. For whoever would save his life will lose it, and whoever loses his life for my sake will find it. For what will it profit a man, if he gains the whole world and forfeits his life" (Matthew 16:24-26).

In 1994, Jesus began to call me into ministry to the poor and the homeless, but He first needed to change my heart. For years, I had felt no responsibility to help the poor because I thought that it was the duty of the government and Churches to help the needy. During this time, I read Isaiah 58:7, which tells us to share our bread with the hungry and bring the homeless poor into our houses. The Father began to put compassion in my heart for those in need. The Father removed my cold selfish heart and replaced it with the heart of Jesus. I started to take the homeless off the street and put them into my 1961, ten by fifty-five-foot mobile home. At one point, I had a complete family of five sleeping in my home. During this time, my pastor asked me, "What if God has called you to inner-city ministry?" I answered that I didn't think that the Lord would ever take me away from the place that I loved—I did not yet know God's plan for my life. The Church was planning a three-day trip to a large city for a pastor and leadership conference. I had not been to a city in about seventeen years, and I resisted going with them for several weeks. My plan was to buy a house and live the rest of my life in the mountains, but God's plan was to call me to inner-city ministry. The Lord showed me that my goals were selfish, and He asked me how I could justify spending all my money on myself when people where perishing without Christ. He called me to leave the comfort of the mountains and follow Him to a city to minister to the homeless. I had saved up money for seven years when the Lord asked me to give it all away to the poor and follow Him. By the Grace of God, I was able to obey His call and leave everything behind to follow Christ.

I have learned to obey the call of the Holy Spirit and never look back. Several years later, I returned to these same mountains for a vacation, but the Joy of God's presence was gone—the Spirit had moved on, and so must I. The Scriptures teach us to forget what lies behind and press on to what lies ahead. Moses was once faced with a decision to go into the promised land without God's presence, or to stay in the wilderness with the Spirit. He decided to stay in the desert with the Father (Exodus 33:12-16). I have also decided to go only where the Father leads me. God's Spirit fills us with Joy when live in obedience to Him. David writes, "Thou dost show me the path of life; in thy presence there is fullness of joy, in thy right hand are pleasures for evermore" (Psalm 16:11). God is my everything—I will not look back.

I followed Christ down to the city thinking that I was coming back in three days—but God had other plans. During my visit, I came across a Christian homeless program, and Jesus called me to stay with them in their discipleship house. I didn't know anyone in the area, but I trusted God to take care of me. I was obedient to the call of Christ for the past twenty-five years ministering to those in need. God has been faithful and has provided for me all these years.

Peter Schuler

A man's steps are ordered by the LORD... Prov. 20.24

I was given the heart of Jesus to unconditionally love the outcasts of society and treat them as if they were Jesus. Jesus taught me to serve the least of these without judging them. The Lord opened doors for ministry, and I preached the Gospel on the streets at four discipleship programs, missions, nursing homes, and nine jails and prisons. I found the joy of being a faithful servant to the call of Jesus. Many were brought to the Lord and saw the glory of God. I offered my life as a living sacrifice, and God's Love has poured out through me to those in need. Like Peter on the Mount of Transfiguration, I had desired to stay on the mountain with God, but I had been called to the valley where many were lost in sin. We have all been commissioned by Jesus to go into all the world and make disciples of all nations (Matthew 28:18-29).

I will never regret the decision to follow Christ, and it has been a blessing to watch the Holy Spirit work great miracles in people's lives. The Father has called each one of us to spread His Love to others. If we reject His call, we will miss the mighty works that the Lord has planned to do through us. I have decided to devote the rest of my life sowing into people instead of seeking my own personal gain. I offered my life to the Father and prayed that the Lord would use my life as a humble vessel through which His Love can flow to others. My life has meaning only when I am a servant walking in love. I pray that the Lord removes all selfishness from my heart and replaces it with the heart of Jesus. I pray, "Lord, love the world, seek the lost, brokenhearted and afflicted through me and let me always see the outcasts of this society through Your eyes of Love."

Shortly after I arrived in the city, I was anointed by the Holy Spirit to preach and teach the Gospel. The Lord spoke to me, "The Spirit of the Lord is upon me, because He has anointed me to preach the good news to the poor. He has sent me to proclaim release of the captives and recovering of sight to the blind, to set at liberty those who are oppressed, to proclaim the acceptable year of the Lord" (Luke 4:18-19). Jesus revealed to me that no person or spirit would ever be able to stop this anointing. These verses perfectly describe the next twenty-five years of ministry. The Holy Spirit anointed me to preach the Gospel to the poor and proclaim release of those who were captive to sin, addictions, fear, and despair. The Spirit moved through me to overcome spiritual blindness in many people so that they could see the Light of the Gospel and turn to Jesus to be saved.

Peter Schuler

The Spirit set many free who were oppressed by the enemy and spiritual darkness. When the Lord revealed to me that He had called me to preach and lead worship services, I had to trust God and overcome my severe fear of speaking and singing in front of people. The Lord soon opened doors for me to teach a one-hour Bible class at the discipleship program. I was afraid, and it seemed like there was a large Goliath of fear standing in front of me, telling me that I would fail. I stood up, trusted God, and His strength was made perfect in my weakness. I began to teach several Bible classes a day and lead many worship services every week. All glory goes to Him because I know this ministry came from Him. I simply stepped out by faith and let the Holy Spirit speak and sing through me. I do not seek my own words, but I pray for the Spirit to give me the message. The Scriptures clearly state that we need not worry about what we are to say because it is not us who speaks, but the Holy Spirit speaking through us (Luke 12:11-12). My words have no power, but His Word brings healing and life to those who hear. I pray before every service for the Holy Spirit to speak His words to His people. I also relied on the Spirit leading me to do hundreds of hours of counseling to the homeless and to the incarcerated.

Twenty-five years ago, my pastor asked me to take a teacher from the women's ministry to a jail service. This teacher later became my wife. This was our first "date," and for the next seven years, we sang and taught together in jails, prisons, discipleship programs, missions, and nursing homes. It was a glorious time of ministering in the power of the Holy Spirit. One pastor at the program called our marriage "a match made in heaven." After seven years, my wife decided to leave

Warrior for Christ | Call of Jesus into Ministry

Trust in the LORD for ever, for the LORD GOD is an everlasting rock. Isaiah 26:4

the ministry and work full time. It hasn't always been easy, but by God's grace, we have been married for over twenty years.

Jesus has been faithful to do many miracles during the past twenty-five years of ministry. In the late nineties, The Lord called me to do several weekly nursing home services. One Sunday, as I was preparing for the service in the Chapel, a lady in a wheelchair told me that a terminal patient down the hall had been unplugged from life support and he had been expected to die several days earlier. She believed that there was a reason that he was still alive. I went into the room, and the man was lying motionless on the bed. The Holy Spirit told me to lead him in a sinner's prayer, even though he couldn't physically respond. I prayed with him and then asked the Lord to take him with angels to Heaven. His two daughters were in the room, and I asked them if they were believers. They told me that they didn't know Jesus and I led both of them to Christ. I returned to the Chapel, and the lady in the wheelchair joined us several minutes later and told me that the man had just passed away. She stayed for the service and gave her life to Christ during the altar call. She passed away several weeks later. God's Word promises that He works in all things for good and brings life out of apparent tragic situations. It has been a privilege to minister to these precious people—many who were on their way to meet Jesus. I have seen crippled people in wheelchairs stand up with the Power of the Spirit of God. One man in a nursing home, who had not spoken or moved for seven years, began to sing, talk, and laugh when we sang "Amazing Grace." During this time, the Father began to give me His love for patients in nursing homes. He filled my heart with His grief for the elderly that were perishing without Him. I realized that He loved them more than I could ever know. He showed me that His Spirit had tried to draw them to Christ for their entire lives, but many were resisting His love to the very end. One day, I remember wheeling a very thin woman in a wheelchair to our service. She looked up at me and said, "I'm dying," and I replied, "You need Jesus." She shouted "No, No, take me back to my room." In sorrow, I took her back and she passed away a short time later. The Father loved her so much, but she didn't want Him. Many times, my heart has been broken with God's love for the lost who are perishing. He sent His Son to die on the Cross for all of us—what more could He do?

The Word of God has tremendous Power to change lives. I remember teaching a message at a discipleship program on forgiveness. After the class, one of the students confided to me that he had intended to commit suicide later in the day, but he had changed his mind when the Holy Spirit spoke to his heart through the message on forgiveness. He had already written a suicide note and planned to leave his wife and several children, but God spoke to him to forgive. I have gone to the deathbed of a friend with AIDS who was in the ICU for spinal meningitis. His blood cell count was very low, and we were told that he was dying. When I arrived, the Holy Spirit directed me to tell him the story of King Hezekiah's healing and that God was going to give him another fifteen years of life (see Isaiah 38:1-5). The Lord healed him according to His Word and extended his life. I have seen the Spirit moving so powerfully in a room full of inmates that all of them were on their knees before God while we sang, "We are standing on Holy Ground." God has graciously used me to guide hundreds of men and women to Him, and I have witnessed many healings. I was only the vessel that God used by His grace, and I will never take any credit for the ministry. To Him be all the glory!

Jesus still does the same miracles today as He did in the time of the Gospels. One Sunday, we planned to do two services, and we brought about one hundred and ten communion cups which included wafers. We went to the prison and gave out about seventy-five cups, and then drove to the jail to do the next service. In this section of the facility, the inmates slept in tents and spent the day in an indoor facility. We usually had about thirty inmates attend our service, but this time the guard announced that the prisoners could either go outside in the one-hundred-and-five-degree heat or go to Church. Seventy inmates attended our service—with only thirty-five communion cups. I read an account of the Last Supper in 1 Corinthians 11:23-26 and distributed the cups. The thirty-five cups multiplied to provide enough for seventy men with two left over, like the miracle of the loaves and fishes (John 6:5-14). Years later, inmates who witnessed this event were still talking about this miracle.

For many years, I have been called to evangelize on the streets and in the jails. I have seen the Father do amazing miracles to bring sinners to Christ. The Holy Spirit anointed me to lead people to Christ in cars, fast food restaurants, parking lots, city streets, alleys, city parks, jails, and nursing homes. I learned to be sensitive to the leading of the Spirit and not to lean on my own understanding. In the late 1990s, I chose to ride my bicycle from the Discipleship House where I resided to a park several miles away. Later in the afternoon, I returned to the Discipleship House and I heard the Spirit tell me to ride back to the park. At first, I objected because I had just come from there, but I obeyed the Spirit. I arrived at a small pond, and I saw a teenage boy on a dock waving his hands. I concluded that the Spirit wanted me to share the Gospel with him. He was seeking answers after both of his parents had recently died. I had the privilege of leading him to Christ. There have been many amazing encounters with the homeless during the street outreaches. I once told a homeless man that Jesus loved him, and he began to weep and hug me for about twenty minutes. He replied that no one had loved him in his entire life. He accepted Christ and his heart was filled with God's Eternal Love.

During this time, I met a seventy-two-year-old man who was incarcerated for the first time in his life. I began sharing the Gospel with him, and I realized that he had never been told by his Church that he needed to be born again. This man had spent his whole life in Church, and no one had told him the first step—how to have a personal relationship with Christ. I prayed with him, and I watched the Holy Spirit bring eternal life into him. The Father had brought him to jail to hear the true Gospel and be saved. Unfortunately, there are many who are lost in Churches. Later, I met a challenging lady in a wheelchair who had lived for years on the street or in a homeless shelter. She was frequently angry, arguing and yelling at people. The love of Jesus reached her when she became terminally ill with lung cancer. She gave her life to Christ, and it was a privilege to hold her hand as she passed away and was raised up with angels to meet Jesus. With God, all things are possible.

I learned not to judge others by outside appearances. One Sunday afternoon, I was ministering at one of our street outreaches and praying for the Holy Spirit to lead me to the right person. As I prayed, a "drug dealer/pimp" pulled up in a Cadillac with two prostitutes in the back. He got out of the car and acted like he didn't want to be at the outreach. The Spirit told me that he was ready to hear the Gospel. I talked to him, and he told me that he wasn't homeless like the other people at the outreach. I said, "But you need Jesus." He replied with tears that He wanted to accept Jesus as his Lord and Savior. The Father knew that his heart was ready, despite the way he appeared to me on the outside.

The Lord often showed me His amazing grace. One of the disciples in our program returned to his old life on the street. Several times, I would find him homeless and hungry, and I would take him to get food at a restaurant. The last time I saw him was at another homeless ministry where I was teaching. He told me that he would die if he went out again and used drugs. They found him stabbed to death in a field, and his brother asked me to do the memorial service.

Peter Schuler

I wanted to speak the truth at the service, and I prayed for several days asking God whether he had been saved. The Lord answered that He had been merciful and had taken him home before he crossed the line. The Scriptures say that God does not wish that any would perish. The family was angry at him, and I was unable to persuade anyone to speak on his behalf at the service. They did not believe that he went to heaven until I preached a message on grace and forgiveness. His brother stood up and said that he was saved through his brother. The Lord led me to give an altar call and eleven members of his family gave their lives to Christ. God's grace is truly amazing.

The Lord called me to help find housing for hundreds of homeless. I helped one sixty-five year-old Vietnam veteran move into his first home in his entire adult life. Later, he helped to distribute food boxes to hundreds of people. I helped a sixty-two-year-old man find an apartment after he had lived on the street for twenty-five years. He had not slept indoors for twenty-five years, and he spent the first two weeks sleeping in the parking lot. After he adapted to his new home, he stayed in his apartment for many years and had no intention of going back to the street. I brought some apartment owners and managers down to the homeless shelter to sign people up for housing. There was a high vacancy rate at the time, and the apartment building owners were willing to let them move in for seventy-nine dollars. It has been a joy to provide housing for so many hurting people who had been suffering on the street. Many told me that they had lost hope of ever finding a home. God made a way for many of His children to experience the joy of living in their own apartment. Jesus has led me to find housing for a whole family of five who were living on the street. I often did regular follow-up visits to the new tenants and brought them food boxes. I helped house many homeless with addictions and serious mental and physical illness, and I often connected them to services. Unfortunately, I had to stop assisting the homeless two years ago when my vertebrae fractured. I am thankful for the years I spent helping those in need, and I will always love God's children who are living on the street.

The Lord gave me great grace and boldness to preach the Gospel. I was on an outreach in the "Zone," which was one of the most violent areas of town. There was a group of men in a circle selling crack, and I slipped into the circle and put my flyer that said in bold letters "Jesus Loves You" on top of the drugs. I spent almost ten years evangelizing and outreaching to the homeless alone on Friday nights in many different city parks. Some were gang members and others were high on drugs and alcohol. I handed out lunches and showed them God's love. I was told by one person that they saw angels protecting me as I walked across the park. Jesus has delivered me from some difficult situations involving guns and knives. When we are called by Jesus, He covers us with His grace. All glory goes to Him.

Sometimes the Lord calls us to evangelize when it appears inconvenient to us. Years ago, I was busy at work, and I stopped at a store to buy some supplies. I saw a young man who I had taken off the street and into my home. The Spirit told me to share the Gospel with him, but I was hesitant because he had stolen from me, and I was busy. I soon realized that his soul was worth far more than the money that I lost and the few minutes I would spend talking with him. I shared the good news of the Gospel with this man, and by the Grace of God, he accepted Christ.

Peter Schuler

It has been a privilege to be used by Jesus to bring hundreds of souls into the kingdom. They were considered outcasts of society: "drunks," "bums," "addicts," "drug dealers," "pimps," "gang members," "hardened criminals," and "chronically homeless." Society considered them worthless and useless, but in God's eyes, they were His beloved children who had come home to Him. All Heaven rejoiced as these lost souls, who were often rejected and hated by this world, entered into God's kingdom. I have seen Jesus save rival gang members who spent many years at war with each other. They were now at peace and brothers in Christ. The Lord has commanded His servants to go out quickly to the streets and lanes of the city and bring in the poor, maimed, blind, and lame, that His house may be filled (Luke 14:21-23). The Lord is calling the weak, the outcasts, and the hated in this world to come to Him and live forever in His Kingdom. God chose what is foolish, weak, low, and despised in this world to be people and live with Him forever. (1 Corinthians 1:26-29). What an honor it has been to love these precious people. Jesus will reward all those who love, serve, and give to those in need.

Unfortunately, the poor and needy of this world are often rejected by the Church. Some years ago, I brought a friend from our homeless discipleship program to a Church service. He was homeless with emotional problems and was covered with tattoos. We sat down in the middle of the Church and listened to the pastor teach on compassion and reaching out and loving others who were different from us. As we sat in the service, everyone around us gradually began to move away from us, and we were left alone in the middle of Church. They formed a twenty-foot "donut hole" around us. As we walked out, no one would greet him and he turned to me and said, "I don't think they like me." The Church was doing exactly the opposite of what the pastor was teaching and what the Word of God commands us to do. We are called to love those in need and treat them as if they are Jesus. (Matthew 25:40). God did a miracle with this man who was rejected by the Church. He was illiterate and had only a third-grade education. He wanted to read the Bible, so we prayed that God would give him the ability to read. Shortly after our prayer, he went to prison for two and a half years for an old charge. He spent the time learning to read, and by the time he returned to the discipleship program, he had read the Bible seventeen times and could quote scriptures by memory for hours. Amen! God is good. He was rejected by the Church but chosen by God.

Have we been obedient to the Great Commission of Jesus to, "Go therefore and make disciples of all nations, baptizing them in the name of the Father and of the Son and of the Holy Spirit, teaching them to observe all that I have commanded you; and lo, I am with you always, to the close of the age" (Matthew 28:19-20)? It is glorious to be a humble servant that God uses to love those in need. We are commanded by Jesus to humble ourselves, become servants, and put the needs of others before our own. Jesus is our example—He came to serve and not to be served. The love of God was poured out into me through the Holy Spirit, and living waters began to flow out of my heart to those in need. I began to enter into the joy of my Master as I was obedient to His call.

I pray, "Lord, give Your Love for the lost souls of this world and send me out to a world that is perishing. Help me to love them unconditionally, without judgment or condemnation. Let me be Your ambassador to spread Your message of the Good News of the Gospel.

I am not on this earth for my selfish pleasure and enjoyment—I am alive to fulfill Your call upon my life and do the work of the ministry. Lord, here I am, send me (Isaiah 6:8). I am available to do Thy Will. Let me love those who are rejected and hated by this world." (Portions of this chapter are based on my first book, *In Pursuit of God: A Love Story.*)

8 | "Terminal" Cancer

Currently, the Lord has called me to walk by faith with Him through Stage Four incurable cancer. Since 1979, I have often worked as a landscaper, and I frequently used a popular weedkiller. When I came to Phoenix, I continued to work part time as a landscaper as I ministered to the homeless. I learned later that my decades of exposure to the weed killer caused me to develop Non-Hodgkin's Lymphoma (NHL). Several people with NHL and good lawyers have won large jury awards against the manufacturers of this product—although they have not yet received any money. About thirteen years ago, I was spraying this pesticide in a yard using a five-gallon container. I opened the sprayer not realizing that it was still pressurized. The weed killer sprayed into my face and I passed out when my brain went black. I did not pass out from lack of oxygen, but it felt like someone turned off my brain. At the time, this product was considered safe, but I now knew from personal experience that it was dangerous. I stopped landscaping shortly after this incident—I never wanted to touch the chemical again. Shortly after this experience, I began to have skin cancer in five places on my face, and three surgeons did several operations to remove the cancer. The doctors now estimate that my lymphoma started in 2011, which was one to two years after I was sprayed in the face.

I gradually I began to feel symptoms of fatigue and sinus problems. The cancer in my bone marrow gradually caused deterioration of my back and hips. A doctor told me during this time that my right hip was so bad that it was a "twelve out of ten." My left hip has now also deteriorated. I continued to hike in the mountains, but the pain was so severe that I was nearly paralyzed by the end of the day. I fought for years to keep going, but I gradually lost the battle. For a while, I continued to ride my bicycle using my left leg only because of the severe pain in my right leg. Eventually, the pain caused me to completely stop riding my bicycle and my motorcycle. I had chronic sinus issues, and my primary care physician diagnosed it as anemia and a sinus infection. I was given several anti-biotics which did not improve the symptoms. The doctor maintained that the sinus infection would go away on its own.

I was not correctly diagnosed until 2017, when my surgeon sent me to get a biopsy of an enlarged lymph gland in the groin area (near my right hip that had been deteriorating). The biopsy showed that I had Non-Hodgkin's Lymphoma (NHL), and I went to the Cancer Treatment Centers of America where the oncologist did multiple CT and PET scans and blood tests over a two-month period.

They determined that I had a rare form of Stage Four Non-Hodgkin's Lymphoma called Waldenstrom—there are only 1,100 to 1,500 cases in the US per year. Note: Waldenstrom is often scored on a point system instead of stages, but my doctor referred to my case as Stage Four. The cancer was in my blood, in numerous lymph nodes in my body, and in 50% of my bone marrow. Waldenstrom also causes a build-up of proteins which thickens the blood and can lead to heart problems and strokes. Later, I went back to the primary care doctor to inform him of the diagnosis, and he replied that he had a vague memory of that disease from medical school. It is unfortunate that I was not correctly diagnosed until I was Stage Four. I continued to work for several years after the diagnosis, outreaching the homeless and connecting them to housing, food, and other services. I tried to glorify God in the midst of cancer, and by God's grace, I received an award in 2018 for "employee of the year" during this time of illness.

I was in shock after my initial diagnosis, and I decided to research Waldenstrom on the Internet. My anxiety increased when I discovered that my type of cancer was incurable and that people had started making plans for my funeral service. This fear was weighing me down, and I needed to turn the cancer over to Jesus. When I was first diagnosed, I heard a lying voice, which I recognized later as the devil, telling me to give up and to prepare to die. He said that I had served God for twenty-five years, and now it was time to go home. In the midst of pain, this sounded appealing. I struggled with this for several weeks, but then I realized that the Lord had called me to live on this earth to serve Him one day at a time. I didn't know about tomorrow, but I knew that I am alive today and the Lord will decide how long I will live in this world. The Word teaches us not to worry about tomorrow but focus on following Christ today (Matthew 6:34). The Holy Spirit gave this Cancer Motto to me, which has given me much peace and strength.

My Cancer Motto:
Give it to God,
Live one day at a time,
and try to help as many people as I can every day.

I began to realize that I needed to give everything to Jesus and let Him bear the burden of the cancer. Jesus asks us to "Come to me, all who labor and are heavy laden, and I will give you rest." (Matthew 11:28). Jesus has carried me through every step of this cancer journey—through the pain and the long road to walking again. I spent my time praying rather than worrying as the Bible teaches, "Have no anxiety about anything, but in everything by prayer and supplication with thanksgiving let your requests be made known to God. And the peace of God, which passes all understanding, will keep your hearts and minds in Christ Jesus" (Philippians 4:6-7). When I focused on Jesus, He took away the anxiety and replaced it with a peace that comes only from the Holy Spirit. Like the eye of the hurricane, there is a place in the midst of the storm where we are in perfect peace: "Thou dost keep him in perfect peace, whose mind is stayed on Thee, because he trusts in thee" (Isaiah 26:3). Jesus gave me peace in my heart, and I began to give Him thanks in the midst of suffering.

With the Lord's help, I now had the strength to face the cancer treatment. My doctor at CTCA decided to put me on Rituxan and a

Bendamustine infusion once a month. I had a severe reaction to the Rituxan, and the infusions had to be stopped numerous times during every session. It raised my heart rate, caused rashes, and severe nausea. My wife shouted, "You are killing my husband." The nurse added to the stress when she printed an article from the Internet which explained the connection between the medicine and the mustard gas used by the Nazis in World War II. Of course, this information did not help my anxiety level.

Note: This was the nurse's last day on the job, and this medicine is obviously not mustard gas, but it is a strong medicine. The nurses wore suits and lead-lined gloves when they infused it into me. The infusions took nine and a half to ten hours because of my adverse reactions.

Note: Many people do not have the same negative reactions to this medicine. I continued to work during this time, although I needed to take off the first three to five days after treatment because of fatigue. For several days, I could only eat chicken noodle soup and bread. Slowly, I regained my health, and I felt fairly good at the end of the month until I went in for another infusion.

The doctor took me off the medicine several months later because it wasn't effective—it had only dropped my IgM level from 3,200 to 2,700. This blood test measures the protein level in my blood, which is an indicator of whether the treatment is working. The normal level is less than two hundred. The doctor decided to put me on Imbruvica, which was an oral chemotherapy drug that cost thirty thousand dollars per month for those without insurance—that is one thousand dollars a pill! The price today is about half that amount. The medicine brought my IgM blood levels from 2,700 down to about 600, and I was able to keep working for the next two years. I took several rest days a month because of the fatigue. My job finding housing for the homeless became increasingly stressful and complicated when they required us to fill out over twenty clinical documents for each client. I worked about an extra two hours a day completing progress notes without being reimbursed for the overtime. They knew about my Stage Four cancer, but they still required me to bring in ten thousand dollars of income per month. I was told later that one of the supervisors had stated in a staff meeting that they were "working Peter to death." The supervisors kept pressuring us to make more money. They fired many employees who were not bringing in the required amount of income, and also those who had high medical expenses. My supervisor often advised me to retire, and I was forced to put in long hours to be a top producer on the team so that I could keep my job and my health insurance. The cancer was getting more severe, and I was feeling increasingly fatigued from the stress and the increased workload.

From the beginning of my treatment, I was concerned that the cancer could damage my back. The CT scan showed at least one lesion on my back, and 50% of my bone marrow was cancer. I was told by the medical staff who conducted my scans that my bones "lit up like a Christmas tree." I discussed this issue multiple times with my oncologist, who stated that the cancer would not damage my bones. Unfortunately, a year and a half later, the cancer resulted in the massive deterioration of my spine. When my back collapsed, the doctor continued to maintain that the cancer did not cause the damage. The surgeon and other doctors disagreed with him, but he would not listen to them either. I requested to be transferred to

another doctor, but after several months, they could not seem to find a suitable replacement.

I finally decided to move to another job within the same company, where I helped inmates successfully transition from jails into treatment programs and halfway houses. This job was also challenging because we were working with career criminals—some with over two hundred arrests. I was so exhausted from the workload of the previous job that in a couple weeks, I became very sick with pneumonia. This illness can be fatal for NHL patients, and I was in bed for about three weeks on anti-biotics. I recovered from the illness, went back to work, and continued to take the Imbruvica. Several months later, I developed vertigo and I was unable to work for about a month, until the doctors were able to successfully treat the condition. Again, I returned to work for about a month and a half until my vertebrae collapsed. One Sunday, I attempted to get out of bed and there was a sharp pain in my back. Somehow on Monday, I was able to drive with a broken back to my primary care doctor to get an X-ray. For some reason, they were not able to see that I had a severe compression fracture caused by the cancer. This was the same office that misdiagnosed my cancer. The next day, I went to the CTCA hospital, and they did a CT scan and two MRI's (they did two because they had stopped one vertebra short of the fracture on the first scan). The facility did not have the proper back board to move me, and I screamed in pain as four of the staff pulled me up from the flat scanning surface. I was promised pain medication before the scan, but it didn't come until I was back in my room screaming in pain. I believe that their improper techniques of moving me during these scans may have contributed to further damage to my back. Months later, I went to another hospital, they were able to move me without pain using a sheet and a back board. I stayed at the CTCA hospital for several days in extreme pain, waiting for my surgery. I was not able to take much pain medicine because of my severe constipation. Three days later, they performed a kyphoplasty surgery, which involved trying to lift up the collapsed vertebra and then reinforcing it with a cement-like product. The surgeon also used a microwave to attempt to kill the cancer. The pathology test revealed that 90% of my bone marrow was cancerous and that the fracture was caused by the cancer.

After the surgery, the surgeon told me to move as much as possible and wrote a letter to my employer giving me permission to work in seven to ten days. I went to several physical therapy sessions, and the staff had me bend over and stretch my back, which caused more pain and possible damage. The surgery strengthened my L5 vertebra, but the remainder of my vertebrae were weakened by the cancer. Within the next couple months, I endured four fractures of the vertebrae below the surgery, and six fractures of the above vertebrae. My employer was pressuring me to return to work immediately or lose my job. I returned to work after ten days, but the pain increased every day until I could no longer walk. I tried to work from home on my laptop for several days, but my employer would not permit me to continue. Four days later, the company fired me after thirteen and a half years because I had missed too much time from work. I was fired for being sick, two years after receiving an award for being employee of the year.

For about five months, I was forced to sit in a chair because I was unable to walk or lay down in a bed. I was in extreme level ten-out-of- ten pain during this time, and my back was in constant states of muscle spasms and contractions. I remained in the chair day and night, except for one very painful trip to the toilet each morning. I often felt like I was going to pass out from the pain as I walked the six feet from the chair to the toilet. The pain in my back was unbearable, and I was forced to lift myself up with my arms day and night to relieve that pressure on my back. Somehow, I held myself up even in the night when I was asleep. The side arms of my chair were eventually crushed, and they are now held together with duct tape. I developed neuropathy and numbness in my feet and lower legs. During this time, the Lord gave me a vision of the five months I had spent in the chair. In the vision, I was lifted up by the Spirit above my body and looked down at myself sitting motionless. Jesus revealed to me that my body was my prison. I had spent many years ministering to inmates locked up in jails and prisons—some in solitary confinement. I began to have more understanding about what they were experiencing in their isolation. During the time I was confined to my chair in extreme pain, Jesus began to heal the sorrow that was in my heart from the suffering I had experienced during my entire life. For several months the Lord healed my heart as He took me on a journey through all of the events that had caused the sorrow. I gradually began to feel the heaviness lift from me as Jesus set me free. The social worker at the hospital attempted to find a nursing home for me, but none would accept me because the Imbruvica was too expensive. Note: the hospitals and nursing homes do not permit patients to take their own medications. My insurance company would not pay for a caretaker to assist me or for a hospital bed. Fortunately, about six months later, I was able to purchase an adjustable bed and I slept on a bed for the first time in many months—what a blessing! My wife was working eleven hours a day, and I was left alone most of the day. She made me a lunch with an ice pack and set it next to my bed. This was my life for five months. I put my medicine and water on shelves next to my chair. The doctor told me to be patient and take the medication as I "recovered" from the operation. I did not understand why I was in the same amount of pain five months later until I was able to make it to the clinic where they did several scans (I was under anesthesia because of the pain), and they determined that I had suffered ten more fractures of my vertebrae: L1, L2, L3, L4, and L5; T12, T11, T10, T8, T4, T3. The cancer that was in 90% of my bone marrow began to collapse my back. The discs were compressed 20 to 40%, and my backbone was now two inches shorter. I had stenosis, which is a narrowing of the bone around the spinal cord, scoliosis, and multiple discs that had slipped out of place. The doctors decided that my back was too fragile to do any more surgeries. The bone surgeon at the clinic told me, "I am not going to touch your back." I thought, "Only Jesus can fix this." They gave me pain medication and muscle relaxers and sent me home. On the trip home, I screamed in pain when the car when we went over a bump. I prayed hours a day and pleaded for Jesus to show me mercy. By His grace, I started to walk around the house and get my own lunch. Eventually I was able to walk outside every morning with my walker. One day as I walked, the Lord gave me a vision of His Word, coming down out of heaven toward me: "He sent forth His Word and healed them" (Psalm 107:20). As the Word came into me, I remember that it seemed that I was almost hollow inside because I was still very weak. I continued to walk and gain my strength for the next eighteen months.

Peter Schuler

I have been in social isolation for about two years due to the cancer, pain and COVID. I feel like Ezekiel, when God commanded him to stay in his house and He was not allowed to speak except when the Lord opened his mouth to proclaim His word (Ezekiel 3:24-27). The Lord has placed me in my home and opened my mouth to speak His words through Facebook. During this time, the Holy Spirit gave me a vision of my experience of isolation over the past two years. In the vision, I was standing up and giving my testimony of my current and past sufferings, and there were about one hundred people moving around in circles in front of me, but none of them were listening to my testimony. They were too involved with their jobs, families, socializing, and other activities to listen to what I was saying.

My physical social interaction consisted of occasional talks with my wife when she was home from work, and five visits from friends during the past two years. However, the Lord has opened up a door receive support and prayer through many groups on Facebook. I often communicate with people from all over the world. It was difficult to make the transition from my twenty-five years of ministry, where I was focused on people every day, to almost complete isolation. Jesus was always there to carry me through this difficult time. I lost contact with most of my co-workers and clients after my employer took my phone. My ministry to the incarcerated also dissolved when the jail and prison facilities were closed due to COVID over one year ago. A few friends called occasionally when they were driving or had a few free minutes at work. I have forgiven them and moved on with my life. I felt like I was living in a different world as I sat in pain in my chair.

The Imbruvica was effective in lowering my IgM levels, but it can have dangerous side effects. Unfortunately, the Imbruvica caused me to have arrythmia. I had difficulty breathing and I went to my primary care clinic where they sent me immediately to the hospital because my heart rate was one hundred and seventy-six. The hospital spent eight days trying various medications in an attempt to get my heart rate back to normal. Ironically, they were having a difficult time lowering my heart rate because my blood pressure is usually fairly low. They had to be careful with the medicine because it could drop my pressure to a dangerously low level. The nurses hooked me up to wires and had me on twenty-four-hour computerized monitoring. The medicine didn't work, so they tried shocking my heart and then restarting it again. This was effective for only a couple weeks, so they decided to do an ablation surgery where they microwaved the inside of my heart. Thank God, my heart has been stable since the surgery. God is good! During the months of heart issues, my doctors took me off the Imbruvica which caused my IgM blood levels to rise from about 600 to about 4,300. I became increasingly sick with the cancer, but fortunately, I was able to take Imbruvica again when my heart rate returned to normal. At this time, I also developed kidney stones, and they had to do a laser operation. I was at the hospital on Thanksgiving, and I wasn't able to eat anything all day. After the surgery, I developed a urinary tract infection. I went to the surgeon, but he refused to do a blood test and treat it. I suffered from the infection for two and a half months until I could see a new doctor who finally gave me some antibiotics. I talked several times to the supervisor about this doctor, but there was no response.

When I lost my employment, I needed to find another insurance carrier. Fortunately, my wife put me on her insurance, but the employer did not like paying his share of the sixteen thousand dollars per month for the cost of the Imbruvica. The employer decided to save money by switching to an insurance company that didn't cover the Imbruvica prescription. This was a stressful situation because the medicine is necessary for me to live. Fortunately, there was a fantastic advocate who worked for the new insurance provider and found a way for me to continue to take the medicine.

I could barely walk when I was released from the hospital, but my strength returned as I walked every morning with my walker. As I exercised, I prayed with my mind and in the Spirit for my healing, and for others who were suffering. I went back to the jails and resumed my ministry for about two months until the facilities were closed by the COVID virus. Throughout my life, whenever I was beat down, Jesus has reached out His hand and lifted me up. All glory goes to Him!

Fortunately, I now have a new oncologist who understands that the cancer caused the fractures in my back. He has changed my chemo treatment to Brukinsa because he is able to give me a higher dose. Unfortunately, he can't repair the previous damage, but he is focusing on treatment that will stop further degeneration of my bones. I want to commend the Cancer Treatment Centers of America for their kindness and generosity to me. Although I have had some differences with some of the staff, I have also met some wonderful doctors, nurses, and administrative employees at the facility. I am thankful for CTCA. We live in an imperfect world, and sometimes doctors make mistakes. I believe that it is important that we forgive, maintain a positive attitude, and move on with our lives.

9 | Overcoming Cancer by the Resurrection

The Lord gave me a vision of the resurrection power of Christ twenty-five years ago on the front lawn of the Church that I was attending. The Holy Spirit filled me with so much power that it felt like my earthly body could not contain it. I was lifted up in the Spirit, and I looked down to see my body still standing on the ground. I believe that this is a vision of our resurrection when Christ returns. It is difficult to explain the feeling of being filled with the glory and power of the all-knowing, all-powerful, eternal God. The power of the Spirit in me was much stronger than any enemy, including sickness and death. I felt like nothing could come against me. It was an amazing experience that gave me hope through the years of suffering. This is probably the most amazing and powerful vision that the Lord has given me. There is a day when Jesus will return, and God will wipe away every tear, death, pain, sickness, and sorrow (Revelation 21:1-5). No more pain! No more cancer! No more sickness! Hallelujah!

The Word of God declares that the resurrection is both a future event and a daily living reality. Every day, the Father calls me to rise up out of my terminal cancer and walk by faith. We pray for God to remove the sickness, but He may be calling us to overcome it by trusting Him. Jesus declares, "I am the resurrection and the life; he who believes in me, though he die, yet shall he live, and whoever lives and believes in me shall never die. Do you believe this?" (John 11.25-26). The enemy speaks death into me through Stage Four cancer and severe back pain, but Jesus speaks life into me, and I stand up by faith and walk with Him in the resurrection power of Christ. I choose not to submit to the lies of the enemy, but I stand up by the power of God's Word. I walk with Jesus in heavenly places above the death, sickness, pain, discouragement, and depression. The Lord renews my strength every day as the Scriptures declare, "Even youths shall faint and be weary, and young men shall fall exhausted; but they who wait for the Lord shall renew their strength, they shall mount up with wings like eagles, they shall run and not be weary, they shall walk and not faint" (Isaiah 40:30-31). Our own strength will fail, but Jesus will carry us through every storm, because with God all things are possible. The Lord will bring me though this cancer and the pain, and by His grace, I will finish the race set before me.

Every day, Jesus raises me up in His resurrection power to walk above the sickness, pain, depression, discouragement, loneliness, and despair. I seek to keep my eyes on Jesus and walk with the Supernatural God above the water. Like Peter I often sink when I take my eyes off of the Lord, but He is always faithful to lift me up when I cry out to Him (see Matthew 14:23-33). By faith, I am able to do the impossible and overcome cancer because with God, all things are possible. Faith pleases God and brings glory to His name (Hebrews 11:6). What a privilege it has been to walk with the awesome, all-powerful, all-knowing Eternal Creator of the Universe. My faith has been tested by a crippling injury, a terminal illness, and severe pain from incurable cancer, but Jesus has always given me grace and has carried me through the suffering. I draw strength from the living waters of the Holy Spirit to glorify God by bearing fruit in adversity (Jeremiah 17: 7-8; Galatians 5:22-23). Throughout history, God has called men and women to live by faith and trust His plan for their lives. Some men and women of great faith were called to overcome adversity, win victories, and receive healing while others with similar faith glorified God by enduring suffering, adversity, and even death (Hebrews 11:32-40). We become a source of strength, inspiration, and the light

of Christ to others when we walk by faith in victory with the love, joy, peace, and patience of the Holy Spirit.

The Bible teaches us to speak in faith to the mountains in our life to be removed. Every morning when I walk, I speak to the cancer in my blood, bones and lymph glands to be removed in Jesus's name. I speak to my vertebrae to be straightened and returned to their proper position, my bones to become strong, my hips and knees to be restored, and my discs to be healed in the name of Jesus. I declare that my mental capabilities, memory, teeth, and eyes are healed in Jesus's name. I command the pain, neuropathy, sickness, and death to leave my body in the name of Jesus. "Truly, I say to you, whoever says to this mountain, 'Be taken up and cast into the sea,' and does not doubt in his heart, but believes that what he says will come to pass, it will be done for him" (Mark 11:23). I confess this by faith and wait for the healing in God's perfect time.

By faith we realize that the same power of the Holy Spirit that raised Christ from the grave is also in us who believe! Paul prayed for the Church in Ephesians, that their eyes of faith would be opened so that they could see that the same immeasurable power of God that raised Christ from the dead was in them (Ephesians 1:16-23). By grace we have been saved through faith, and He has made us alive together with Christ and raised us up with Him to be seated in heavenly places (Ephesians 2:5-6). I saw a vision twenty-six years ago of an open door into heaven, and Jesus called me to come up to Him into heaven. This was similar to John's vision in Revelation 4. The Holy Spirit lifted me up, and I saw God on the throne. The Father revealed to me that I was called to live in heavenly places before His throne through the resurrection power of Christ. The Lord told me to read and preach the Word, pray, and worship in heavenly places by the Spirit. When we walk with Jesus, our words, prayers, and actions have His authority. Our physical bodies will still be on this earth, but we will live in heavenly places though Christ. When we walk with Him, His Words become our words, His prayers become our prayers, and we worship Him in Spirit and truth. I walk by faith every day with Jesus in heavenly places, above the cancer and pain.

The Bible teaches that there will be a future resurrection of the Church when Christ returns, and our earthy bodies will be changed into a glorified body like Christ's body: "But our commonwealth is in heaven, and from it we await a Savior, the Lord Jesus Christ, who will change our lowly body to be like his glorious body, by the power which enables him even to subject all things to himself" (Philippians

3:20-21). At the last trumpet, Jesus will change us into His image in a twinkling of an eye (1 Corinthians 15:51-56). God promises to make all things new and to purify our hearts and minds from of the effects of sin. We will never have a sinful thought or desire throughout eternity. We are called to trust God in this life as we wait for this blessed hope of a future resurrection, where there will be no sickness, pain, or suffering. I set my hope in Jesus and the vision that He will heal me, for I look not to the things that are seen like cancer and pain, but to the eternal things which are invisible.

10 | A New Ministry

Jesus has gradually given me strength to walk after the collapse of my vertebrae. About eight months after my initial back surgery, I took my walker and returned to the jails to do Church services and one-on-one counseling. When I first talked to the inmates, they informed me that they had been very worried about me after I had disappeared eight months earlier due to my illness. They wrote letters ("tank orders") to the Chaplain and the jail administration, trying to determine what had happened to me. I had rarely missed a service and they were concerned. They prayed fervently, and I could feel the power of their prayers during my illness. There was a great reunion with the inmates when I resumed my ministry. The Holy Spirit works in a powerful way in these services, and the Lord has been doing a mighty work in their lives. The inmates have their own daily Bible studies and prayer meetings, and their daily fellowship resembles that of the early Church. Unfortunately, the jails closed to visitors about two months later due to COVID. At the time of this writing, I am expecting to return to jail ministry again. God has made a way!

I prayed for Jesus to open up a new ministry to me, after the cancer had taken away my job working with the homeless and COVID stopped my services at the jail. God arranged for me to meet a new friend Chuck Keels who encouraged me to open an account on Facebook. At first, I was apprehensive about social media, but I took a step of faith and I soon discovered that Jesus was opening a door for ministry. I set up a profile and joined many prayer, Bible study and cancer support groups. The Holy Spirit led me to pray for many people suffering from cancer and other illnesses, and I sent them messages of hope and encouragement. I shared my testimony of healing with those who had terminal illnesses. The Lord led me to pray for marriages, spiritual protection, financial issues, jobs, housing, and healing from physical and mental health issues. I prayed for individuals, Churches, cities and countries. I taught young believers about the Bible, how to study the Scriptures, and I shared the Gospel with many who were seeking answers. The Spirit led me to post Christian messages and Bible study videos on Facebook. When I first viewed the videos, I realized that my mental capabilities and my speech were slowed down dramatically due to the cancer and the medication. I asked Jesus to take away the pain, and hundreds of believers from all over the world were praying for my healing. By the grace of God, I was able to go about five months without any pain medication. The Lord began to restore my memory of the Bible and my ability to teach the Word. I received many friend requests from pastors and other believers in Pakistan, Africa, India, and Europe. Jesus opened doors for me to do Church services using Facebook in Pakistan, India and other countries.

I thank God every day for the opportunity to minister to people from all over the world through Facebook, as I spend most of my day isolated in my room due to the pain, mobility issues, and the COVID virus. Praise God! Most of my emotional support comes through Facebook from thousands of believers living all over the world. I have learned the importance of keeping a positive mental attitude on this cancer journey. At first, I thought about what I had lost—career, ministry, hiking, bicycle riding and trips to the mountains. I decided to take captive these negative thoughts, and I chose to be grateful and give thanks every day to God for His blessings. As I learned to be content, the Lord has opened up a whole new ministry and new friends through the Internet. God is good! When God closes one door, He opens another one. I am amazed that I have been able to minister to thousands of people from many parts of the world as I continue to be isolated in my room. Thank you, Jesus!

11 | Overcoming Pain

For me, pain is the most difficult adversary and the greatest test of faith. I am currently dealing with eleven fractures in my back: L1, L2, L3, L4, and L5; T12, T11, T10, T8, T4, and T3. Pain has tested me beyond my limits and drove me to rely on Jesus to carry me through many very difficult times. I have previously experienced severe pain during my seven-year illness, when I only had the strength to face it one second at a time. By the grace of God, Jesus carried me through seven years with no health insurance, medical care, or pain medication. I also experienced extreme pain when my hip was broken in twelve places. I cried out to Jesus in prayer, and He was faithful to bring me through the storm. My current pain began in my back, hips and legs about ten years ago, but it became unbearable when my vertebrae collapsed about two years ago. As I described in chapter nine, I lived in a chair for about five months in extreme pain with my back in frequent muscle spasms. The pain was so severe that I had to lift myself up with my arms twenty-four hours a day to take the pressure off of my backbone. Frequently, the level of pain was so extreme that I had to scream, but I was alone in my room and only the Lord heard me. I prayed for hours a day and pleaded for Jesus to show me mercy and heal me like the cripples and lepers in the Bible. There were thousands of people praying for me from many other nations of the world—Pakistan, Africa, India, Europe, and the Philippines. I am very thankful for their prayers. Jesus began to heal me gradually, and I was able to walk short distances with my walker. I was still in pain with every step, but by faith I pushed myself to get better. I have learned that we need to trust Jesus and keep fighting and pushing through the pain as much as possible. There is a balance—I can't lay in bed all day, or I will not be able to move again, but I can't push myself too much and cause damage to my back. Jesus answered my prayer, and I was able to stop taking pain medications for about five months. I recommend to those who are experiencing pain to be careful to limit the amount of pain medication. I drew my strength from Jesus through prayer and took the minimum amount required to keep the pain at a reasonable level. I needed the medication during the times of extreme pain, but I stopped taking the medication when the level of pain became bearable. I could walk in the morning, but I had to stop moving in the afternoon and evening when the pain increased substantially.

My faith was tested again over two months ago, when the extreme back pain returned. For several weeks, I was unable to even walk to my front door. With eleven fractured vertebrae, I have to be very careful with my movements, such as getting up and down from bed and my chair. One wrong movement can put my back out of alignment, which would cause all the muscles in my back to contract. It feels like someone was sticking a knife into my spine. Sometimes, my muscles would lock up when trying to get up out of my chair. I would have to sit down, take a muscle relaxer, and wait about fifteen minutes before I could get up. With eleven compression fractures, stenosis, slipped discs, and many flattened discs, one wrong movement and my whole back would lock up in screaming pain. My wife would drive me to the clinic, and I would frequently scream when we went over a bump in the road. It has been a difficult and discouraging time, but I put my trust in God and praise Him every day. In the midst of suffering, I will give thanks to God for all of His blessings. I trust God every day, not understanding, but believing that He is working in everything for good. I am currently in pain as I write this book, but I will keep going by faith as long as Jesus gives me life. Recently, I sent out another prayer request on Facebook, and 5,200 believers from all over the world began praying for me. I am humbled and grateful for their prayers! By the grace of God, the level of pain has begun to decrease. I am starting to walk every morning, and I am able drive my car to doctor appointments and to the store. Thank you, Jesus!

For those who are experiencing suffering and pain, I would recommend reaching out for support on Facebook. There are groups filled with people who are enduring similar issues of pain and suffering. The members of these groups will support, listen, and pray for those who are suffering. I am walking because of Jesus and the prayers of thousands of faithful believers. God hears the prayers of His saints.

I truly believe that without the prayers and the Divine intervention of Jesus, I would not be alive. All praise, glory and honor go to the Lord!

12 | Why Do We Have to Suffer?

I don't have all the answers, but God does. One thing I have learned is that God is God, and we are not. We overcome by faith and not by having all the answers. The Lord shares what we need to know to trust Him. When I first started to follow Jesus, I asked the Father many questions, and He answered me that one day in heaven, we will meet on a mountain and He will answer all of my questions—but for now, I must live by faith. The will and plan of God is often a mystery to us while we are still on this earth. I can't explain why I have cancer, but I know God is good, merciful, loving, kind, compassionate, patient, and faithful. The Cross is the central theme of the Gospel, and we are called to suffer for Christ (1 Peter 2:21). We don't choose our own path, God does. It helps to put our affliction in perspective: our pain is small compared to what Jesus suffered for us. He took on our pain and the punishment for our sins on the Cross. What do we have to give Him, but our lives? We present our bodies to Him as a living sacrifice, which is our spiritual worship. Paul suffered greatly for Christ, and yet he called our suffering a slight momentary affliction that is preparing for us an eternal weight of glory beyond all comparison. He tells us not to lose heart when our bodies are wasting away, but that we should look to the unseen, which is eternal.

In the midst of suffering, it is sometimes difficult to believe that God loves us and trust that He is working through the adversity for good. Job wrestled with this issue in the book of Job, and he expressed his anger and frustration at the apparent injustice and unfairness of his situation. Many of us can relate to him when we go through pain or tragedy in our own lives. We want to know why this affliction is happening to us. Many people ask, "How can a good God cause or allow suffering in this world?" The Bible teaches that suffering was not part of God's original plan for man in the Garden of Eden. Sickness and death came into this world when Adam and Eve sinned and became separated from God. Through the death of Jesus on the Cross, we have forgiveness and eternal life, and we are restored into a right relationship with God. There is a choice set before us—the wide and easy path of pride and the flesh, or the narrow path of the Cross. On the road to destruction, we indulge our flesh, but on the path of life, we crucify the flesh and lay down our lives to follow Christ (Matthew 7:13-14). No one likes to suffer—even Jesus despised the shame of the Cross. He endured the pain by looking to the joy that was set before Him (Hebrews 12:2). Jesus prayed for strength in the Garden of Gethsemane to obey the will of the Father and suffer on the Cross.

Peter Schuler

Blessed is he whom Thou dost choose and bring near, to dwell in Thy courts! We shall be satisfied with the goodness of Thy house, Thy holy temple! Psalms 65.4

We are also called to take up our crosses and follow Him on the same path the He walked before us. As a youth, I always sought the easier path of self-gain, but when I met Christ, I counted it all as loss to gain Christ. I have enclosed some Scriptures that will help explain God's plan for suffering. We must realize that God's ways are not our ways. God's plan of the Cross is foolishness to the natural mind, but to those who are being saved, it is the power of God (1 Corinthians 1:18). Looking back over my life, I realize that the Lord used the times of suffering to mold and shape me into the image of Christ. I believe we grow the most during the most challenging times of our lives. Often, we must simply trust God's plan for our lives—He is faithful to carry us through the storm.

Biblical Reasons for Suffering
Discipline

God disciplines the sons He loves so that He can set us free from the power of sin and the lusts of the flesh and change us into the image of Christ (Hebrews 12:5-11). The Lord often disciplines us by allowing us to experience the consequences of our actions. For example, David sinned with Bathsheba and killed her husband. He was disciplined for the rest of his life as a result of his sin—the child that was born to Bathsheba died, there was murder and rape in his family, and one of his sons temporarily took the kingdom away from him (2 Samuel 12.1-33). David was humbled by this discipline, and he never again committed a similar sin. Discipline may be painful now, but the Lord uses it to fill us with His holiness and righteousness.

To Rely on God

The Father uses suffering to humble our pride and teach us to rely on Him in all things. We must learn that apart from Christ, we can do nothing (John 15:5). Our sinful nature wants to be like God and have control, but our own decisions always lead us down the road to destruction. The Bible tells us to trust in the Lord with all of our hearts and not to rely on our own insight, and that He will direct our steps (Proverbs 3:5-7). The Father needs to humble our prideful, sinful nature until we learn to rely on Him. Paul writes that he was so utterly and unbearably crushed that he despaired of life itself, but this suffering made him rely not on himself, but on God who raises the dead (2 Corinthians 1:8-10). Paul relied on Christ because he was often pushed to the limits of endurance with beatings, stonings, persecution, hunger, sleeplessness, shipwrecks, and physical ailments.

To Know Christ

All of us began our lives separated from God because of sin. Through Christ, we become born again and begin our journey to know our Creator. At first, we see the Lord through the eyes of our flesh, culture and the world around us. Gradually, we come to truly know Him as we lay down everything at the Cross and let the Lord reveal Himself to us. Through this revelation, we are changed into His image from one degree of glory to the next (2 Corinthians 3:18). We decrease so that He will increase in our lives. I have prayed to know Christ regardless of the cost, and I never want to compromise or become lukewarm. It is a decision that I will never regret. After Paul experienced the glory of Jesus on the road to Damascus, he decided to count everything as loss to gain Christ. He considered knowing Christ of greater value than all that he had once desired in this world (Philippians 2:7-11). When Jesus enters our hearts, He begins to remove everything in us that is not of God so that He can fill every part of our lives. Before his suffering, Job said that he had known about God (religion), but now He truly knew Him (relationship) (Job 42:1-6).

Obedience

The Word of God teaches that the Cross sets us free from the passions of the flesh so we can begin to live according to the Will of God: "Since Therefore Christ suffered in the flesh, arm yourselves with the same thought, for whoever has suffered in the flesh has ceased from sin, so as to live for the rest of the time in the flesh no longer by human passions but by the will of God" (1 Peter 4:1-2). When our sinful nature is nailed to the Cross, it is dead, and we will no longer be enslaved to the temptations and the passions of the flesh (Romans

6:6). When we are crucified with Christ, He now lives in us to obey the Father.

Humility

God disciplines the proud and gives grace to the humble (1 Peter 5:5). Pride is the root of all sin which originated with the devil's rebellion (see Ezekiel 28 and Isaiah 14). David wrote, "Before I was afflicted, I went astray; but now I keep thy word" (Psalm 119:67). Paul stated that he was given a thorn in the flesh, a messenger of Satan, to keep him from being too elated and proud. Three times he asked God to remove this suffering, but Jesus answered that His grace is sufficient, and His power is made perfect in weakness. Paul wrote that he is content with weakness because when we are weak then the Lord is strong (2 Corinthians 12:1-10). The prodigal son began his journey full of pride, but the Lord disciplined him through his circumstances, and he returned to the Father with a humble heart (Luke 15:11-24). During the years I ministered at several discipleship programs, I often tried to rescue those who had left the program and returned to the street, but God revealed to me that He was still working in their lives to humble them so that they would return to Him with a repentant heart.

Spiritual Warfare

The devil prowls around like a lion seeking to devour us and we are told to resist him, firm in our faith, knowing that the same experience of suffering is required of all true believers (1 Peter 5:8-10). When we follow Christ, we will suffer at the hand of the devil, for he will resist all those who seek to do God's will and walk in the Spirit. The disciples of the early Church were anointed by the power

of the Holy Spirit and spread the Gospel to many parts of the world. The devil launched a counterattack of resistance and persecution. Paul was beaten, stoned, whipped, and shipwrecked for Christ. The disciples were imprisoned, persecuted, and eventually martyred for Christ. Jesus warns us to watch at all times, praying that we may have the strength to escape the evil at the end of the age and stand before Him when He returns (Luke 21:34-36).

Testing our Faith

The Father will use trials to test whether our faith is genuine: "In this you rejoice, though now for a little while you may have to suffer various trials so that the genuineness of your faith, more precious than gold may redound to praise and glory and honor at the revelation of Jesus Christ" (1 Peter 1:6-7). The disciples claimed that their belief in Jesus was strong enough to die for Him, but the Lord knew their hearts: "Do you now believe? The hour is coming, indeed it has come, when you will be scattered, every man to his home, and leave me alone" (John 16:31-32). Jesus often called His disciples men of little faith; they were afraid in the storm and lacked the faith to cast out a demon from a child. Later, when they were baptized by the Holy Spirit at Pentecost, they became men of great faith that changed the world. During the time of Exodus, the Lord tested the faith of Israel ten times, and they failed every time: at the edge of the Red Sea when Pharaoh chased them, when they were thirsty and hungry, and at the edge of the Promised land, when they were too afraid of the giants to go into the land. Rather than trusting God, they grumbled and complained and went back to Egypt in their hearts. The Word of God was of no benefit because it didn't meet with faith in the hearers (Hebrews 4:2).

Remove Distractions

Jesus is still calling us today to leave behind everything and follow Him. Many today are like the rich young ruler who loved his money more than Jesus. In another passage, many were invited by God to a wedding feast, but refused to come because they were distracted with the things of this world. Jesus then sent His servants to the homeless and afflicted and they responded to His call (Luke 14:15-24). I believe that Jesus often removes the distractions in our lives to motivate us to turn to the Lord. I have talked to many people who testified that they had ignored God's call on their life for many years until they had lost everything on the street or in jail. The Lord was finally able to get their attention, and they gave their lives to Christ.

Manifest Christ

When we are born again, Christ is born into us, and we are earthen vessels carrying the glory of Christ within us. We must decrease because our flesh (sinful nature) obscures the Light of Christ from shining through us. Paul writes that he was always given up to death for Jesus' sake, so that the life of Jesus may be manifested through him (2 Corinthians 4:7-11). In Daniel 3, Shadrach, Meshach and Abednego went into the furnace where they were refined and set free, and Jesus was manifested in the fire. When we decrease, then others begin to see the glory of Christ shining through us. I pray that God will continue to work in my life so that others will see Jesus in my words, actions, and attitudes.

Bring us Back to God

There are several stories in the Bible which illustrate God's use of suffering to persuade His people to turn back to Him. The Father used a storm and a large fish to bring Jonah to repentance. God called Jonah to preach to Nineveh, but instead he ran from the presence of God and boarded a ship going the opposite direction. God sent a storm to get his attention, but Jonah refused to listen and went to sleep in the bottom of the boat. He was thrown overboard and then swallowed by a fish, but he continued to harden his heart and resist God. Finally, after three days in the belly of the fish, he repented, went to Nineveh, and preached a message which saved the city (see the book of Jonah). The Father used poverty and affliction to cause the Prodigal Son to return to Him with a humble and repentant heart so that the father could bless and restore him (Luke 15:11-24). The Lord is a God of second and third chances. Thank you, Jesus. In my years of service, I have seen hundreds of prodigal sons and daughters come back to Jesus and receive mercy and grace.

From the rising of the sun to its setting the Lord's name is to be praised. Psalm 118.24

Comfort Others

The Lord comforts us in our afflictions so that we will be able to comfort others in their time of suffering (2 Corinthians 1:3-6). In my years of ministry, the Lord has used all my past experiences of suffering and rejection to help comfort and assist those in need. My afflictions have given me more compassion and empathy for those who are suffering. Because of my personal experiences, I have been able to understand how it feels to be homeless, rejected, and ignored by people. For years, I wandered the streets hungry, with rags on as clothes, and no one stopped to help me. Because of my suffering, the Lord has given me a heart of compassion and a passion to help those in need. I realize now that my whole life has been a preparation for my service to the Lord.

Persecution

As we discussed in chapter six, all those who desire to live a Godly life will be persecuted by family, friends, and fellow Christians. Jesus warns that in these last days, many will fall away, betray one another, and hate one another (Matthew 24:10). Because wickedness is multiplied, most men's love will grow cold. We will be hated by all for Christ's sake. We are called to endure persecution and suffering in a world that has fallen away from God. When our faith is in Christ, we will stand strong in the midst of rejection and opposition.

Reward

The sufferings of this time are not worth comparing to the glory that God has prepared for us in heaven (Romans 8:18). Our pain in this life is small when viewed from the perspective of the reward that is waiting for us in heaven. Jesus will test the works of Christians at the Judgement Seat of Christ. On that day, faithful believers will be rewarded with joy and authority in heaven for all that they accomplished on this earth in obedience to Christ (1 Corinthians 3:10-15). The Bible tells us to rejoice when we share Christ's sufferings so that we can be glad when His glory is revealed. We are to look not to the things of this earth that are passing away, but to our heavenly inheritance, where we will spend eternity with the Lord.

13 | Supporting Those Who Are Suffering

> Bear one another's burdens and
> so fulfill the law of Christ
> *Galatians 6:2*

Cancer is a very difficult emotional experience, and those who are suffering will often feel lonely and overwhelmed. They will seek support from family and friends, but it is difficult for those who have never experienced cancer to truly understand the difficulty of the cancer journey. When I was diagnosed with Stage Four incurable cancer four years ago, I could not have envisioned the pain and suffering that I have lived through in the time since. I have received no support from family and very little help from friends, so I turned to Jesus for strength. Without the Lord, I never could have endured this cancer and the pain. Thank you, Lord! People will let us down, but Jesus never will. I believe that the Lord has put me in this situation to learn to be completely dependent on Him, and He has been faithful to carry me every step along the journey. "For we have not a High Priest who is unable to sympathize with our weaknesses, but one who in every respect has been tempted as we are, yet without sin. Let us then with confidence draw near the throne of grace, that we may receive mercy and find grace to help in time of need" (Hebrews 4:15-16). Over the past two years since my back fractures, I have spent hundreds of hours coming to that Throne of Grace to receive mercy and grace. The Lord is patient and kind and always listens to my sorrow and pain.

As I shared in chapter eleven, after about a year social isolation, Jesus opened a door for fellowship, support, and prayer through Prayer and Cancer Support Groups on Facebook. I received assistance from Non-Hodgkin's Lymphoma and Waldenstrom groups. Jesus also opened up a door to pray and support others who were suffering. I received friend requests from all over the world, and I soon had thousands of people praying for my cancer from Africa, Europe, Pakistan, India and the Philippines. Through the prayers of these believers, I became stronger, and I now walk for about thirty minutes a day. It has been amazing to fellowship with believers from all over the world, and they became a wonderful source of support during these difficult times. I would highly recommend Facebook both as a source of support and as an opportunity to help others. I have been privileged to meet several thousand loving and faithful believers from all over the world.

The lack of support from friends has been disappointing—the loneliest seasons in my life have been during the times of greatest need. I have forgiven them and moved on with my life. God healed and blessed Job only after he forgave his friends and prayed for them

(Job 42:10). As I shared in Chapter nine, the Holy Spirit gave me a vision of the isolation that I have experienced over the past two years. In the vision, I was giving my testimony of suffering, but everyone was too involved with their own lives to listen to me. Five friends have visited over the past two years, and a couple of other friends occasionally call. Some friends told me that it was too depressing to listen to me describe my suffering. The COVID pandemic during this time contributed to my isolation for the last fourteen months. I was the most desperate for assistance when I was unable to move from my chair for about five months. My wife was away at work for eleven hours a day, but she left a lunch for me in a container with ice and she cooked my meals, shopped, and took me to doctor's appointments. I don't think I would have survived without her. Thank you! She often has difficulty offering emotional support because the situation became too stressful for her.

How are we to support those experiencing cancer and other illnesses? Jesus calls us to bear one another's burdens to fulfill the law of Christ (Galatians 6:2). When one member of the body suffers, then all suffer (1 Corinthians 12:27). Jesus is the head of the body, and He calls the members of His body to love and care for those who are in pain. Through Christ, we can truly have compassion and empathy for others who in need. For the past two years, I have longed for someone to take the time out of their busy lives and listen to me. Listening is a form of love and heals the broken hearted. In my years of service, Jesus taught me how to comfort the brokenhearted, listen to their pain, and show them that God loves them. There are many "invisible" people who are suffering alone, longing for comfort and support as the world goes quickly by them. Often, those who are suffering the most are receiving the least assistance. A pastor once told me that compassion is not a feeling, but an action. It is not enough that we feel sorry for someone who is suffering; what are we doing to help them? The Lord commands us to give food, drink and clothes to the needy, welcome strangers, and visit the sick and those in jails. We are told to treat them as if they were Jesus. Jesus warns that when we don't help those who are in need, we have failed to do it unto Him. Jesus is calling us to be His hands and feet to reach out to those who are suffering (Matthew 25: 31-46). In the story of the Good Samaritan, several men avoided the person who was in need, but the Samaritan went to him and offered assistance (Luke 10:29-37). We are not called to build a Church and wait for the needy to come to us, but

The earth is the LORD'S, and the fulness thereof, the world and all those who dwell therein. Psalm 24.1

rather, we are called to go out into the world and share Christ's love. There is a story of a man in an apartment building who was angry at God because He didn't provide milk for the poor family who lived next to him. The Lord answered him, "I called you to help them—I put you next to the family and gave you the resources to provide for them." When we reach out and help those in need, we can easily become burdened with their pain and become overwhelmed. During my years of service, I would sometimes become "burned out" because I was carrying the burdens of other people's suffering inside of my heart. The Lord has taught me to let Him love others through me and allow Him to carry the burdens and the sorrow. I was careful to monitor my emotional health so that I knew when I was becoming run down, overwhelmed, and fatigued. I learned to come to Jesus for strength and comfort.

14 | Praising God in the Storm

The most powerful form of worship is praising God in the midst of suffering. With Stage Four cancer and severe back pain, I lift my hands to the Lord and worship Him. With all of my heart and all of my strength, I will give thanks to the Lord God, the Creator of all things. "Praise the Lord! O give thanks to the Lord, for He is good, for his steadfast love endures forever!" (Psalm 106:1). Our natural reaction in suffering is anger, fear, depression, anxiety, and despair. But God's ways are not our ways, and His Word tells us to rejoice, be joyful, and give thanks in the midst of suffering and persecution. Jesus teaches us to be of good cheer in the midst of tribulation, for He has overcome the world. James reminds us to "Count it all joy when we meet various trials, because the testing of our faith produces steadfastness which leads to spiritual maturity

(James 1:2). The Holy Spirit will give us joy and strength in the most difficult times. Peter tells us to rejoice when we share in Christ's suffering so that we may be glad when His glory is revealed. When the disciples were called before the council, imprisoned, and beaten, they left the council rejoicing that they were worthy to suffer dishonor for the name of Jesus (Acts 5:40-41).

I will praise the Lord through every storm for He is good, and His mercy endures forever. I have learned through these times of suffering that it is essential that we maintain an attitude of gratefulness and contentment. The Word commands us to "Give thanks in all circumstances; for this is the will of God in Christ Jesus for you" (1 Thessalonians 5:18). It is easy to become discouraged in times of pain and adversity. We tend to concentrate on what we don't have and what we have lost, instead of being thankful for every blessing of God. Cancer has taken away my job with the homeless, my ministry, hiking in the mountains, bike riding and most of my friends. Yet, I still choose to praise Jesus every day and give thanks for all of His blessings. I will proclaim that God is good, even when I don't understand. When I am in less pain, I go to the park and worship the Lord with my guitar. I try keep a positive and grateful attitude every day. I will take captive every angry, ungrateful, and negative thought to obey Christ. Paul wrote in prison that he had learned to be content in all circumstances—whether he was in prosperity or adversity, he could do all things through Christ who strengthens him (Philippians 4:13).

The enemy tempts those who are suffering to become discouraged, ungrateful, and angry at God, which places us under the bondage of the evil one. In the book of Job, Satan's plan was to tempt Job to

On the glorious splendor of Thy majesty, and on Thy wondrous works will I meditate. Psalm 145:5

become bitter and curse God after he lost his family and all of his possessions in one day. Instead, Job fell on the ground and worshiped God (Job 1:20-22). If we have anger in our hearts toward God, we must come to him and confess our sins, because He will always forgive us. Job was attacked again when the enemy afflicted him with a painful skin disease. Job held fast to his faith and his integrity and refused to blame God. Job wrote down his struggles with his suffering in the rest of the book of Job, but he never lost his trust in God. Unfortunately, Job's wife fell into the devil's trap and became bitter—she told Job to give up, curse God, and die. We please God when we worship God in the midst of great emotional and physical pain and suffering. In Acts, Paul and Silas were beaten and imprisoned for doing the Lord's work. Rather than feeling sorry for themselves, they began to pray and sing hymns to God, and the Holy Spirit shook the building and set the prisoners free (Acts 16:16-39). There is great spiritual power in praising God in the midst of suffering—it breaks the yoke of bondage and the oppression of the enemy.

15 | Victory in Jesus!

At the time of this writing, I am trusting God for His promised healing. Over a year ago I saw a vision of this scripture coming out of heaven into me:

"He sent forth His Word and healed them."
Psalm 107:20

The Lord has delivered me from the oppression and trauma of my childhood and healed me from a crippling hip injury and a terminal seven-year illness. He has been gracious to reveal Himself in such a glorious way and faithful through all the years of my life. I have been blessed to walk with the Father on many mountain tops, through meadows filled with flowers, beside beautiful lakes, and streams. It has been an honor to serve Christ over the past twenty-five years to help those in need. I have trusted the Lord through the cancer storm, and God has been good to me. I thank Him every day for His blessings, and I stand by faith in the victory of Jesus in the midst of the battle. The pain and suffering will not turn me against God! The enemy and his demonic army seek to torment and destroy me, but I am protected by the blood of Jesus and His army of angels who camp around me. I am not alone, there are thousands of believers praying for me. Thank you, Jesus!

The Lord will deliver me from the power of death and this terminal cancer. I believe that our suffering for Christ is not in vain and that there is a reward waiting for us in heaven. Paul wrote these words at the end of his race: "I have fought the good fight, I have finished the race, I have kept the faith. Henceforth there if laid up for me the crown of righteousness, which the Lord, the righteous judge, will award to me on that Day, and not only to me but also to all who have loved His appearing" (2 Timothy 4:7-8).

Visions of Glory and Hope

In the midst of Stage Four cancer and severe pain, I will proclaim the Lord is coming to deliver us from this present evil age and place His people in the safety of His presence forever! The Lord promises that in the midst of these last days of darkness, the light of God will arise, and His glory will be seen upon us (Isaiah 60: 1-30). We are living in the last days when God will fulfill every vision and prophecy. Believers in every age have lived by faith, longing for the day when Christ returns and reigns with His Church in the new heaven and earth. Jesus will soon reward His people with an eternal and glorious Inheritance, and no one will steal their crowns. Jesus will come for

His Bride and rescue all those who are eagerly awaiting Him. The Lord will deliver us from the power of sin, death and evil. He will heal all sickness and pain and wipe away all tears from our eyes (Revelation 21:1-7). This slight momentary affliction is preparing us for an eternal reward beyond all comparison (2 Corinthians 4:17). Jesus is our Deliverer, and He is calling His Church out of the kingdom of this world (Egypt) into a new Heavenly Land. Jesus is shouting: "Let my People go!" and the devil (Pharaoh) is resisting the plan of God. The enemy seeks to keep God's people in slavery to sin and in bondage under the oppression of this present darkness. Behold, the Lord comes to deliver His people from slavery by the power of His blood and take them to His Heavenly Kingdom. Amen, Hallelujah! For twenty-seven years, I have seen visions of the great outpouring of the Holy Spirit, called the Latter Rain, when the power of the Holy Spirit will gather His elect from one end of heaven to the other and prepare the Church for the return of Christ. In one vision, I walked into a hospital, and the power of the Holy Spirit healed everyone. These visions seem even more improbable now as I write this in pain from terminal cancer, but with God all things are possible. God will accomplish all things in His time and according to His will. It is time to lift up our eyes, for our redemption is drawing near. Amen, Hallelujah! Come, Lord Jesus, come!

There is joy in my heart! Thank you, Jesus, for Your love, mercy, compassion, faithfulness, salvation, healing, strength, kindness, patience, and goodness. Thank you for dying on the Cross for us so that we can be forgiven and live in Your presence for eternity. Jesus has defeated the power of sin, sickness, sorrow, and pain. Thank you that you have prepared a place for us to live in Your glory on a new earth that you will create. I am in awe of You, I love You, I will worship You forever! Come Lord Jesus come!

The Lord will rescue me from every evil and save me for His heavenly kingdom (2 Timothy 4:18). Amen!

The Lord promised me three years ago:

"You will rise, Peter,
You will rise above them all."

Recently, He spoke to me:

"You will be the one who rises up, Peter."

When I was in Switzerland, the Lord gave me a vision of hope of the new heaven and earth where we will spend eternity. No sickness or pain! No devil or hate! No more battles with evil! No more cancer! We will be filled with God's glory and love! Amen, Hallelujah! God is good! Come Lord Jesus, Come!

Peter Schuler

Also by Peter Schuler

In Pursuit of God: A Love Story

Forty-one years ago, the Lord put a passion in the heart of Peter Schuler to seek God with all his heart, soul, and strength. By Grace, the Father has revealed Himself to Peter in a glorious way through visions, revelation, and amazing times of fellowship in the Presence of the Lord. Follow Peter's journey to know God as he worships the Father with music and photography on majestic mountain tops and beside beautiful lakes and streams. It is Peter's prayer that this book will inspire others to fall in love with Christ and begin their own journey to know Him. The Father Loves us more than we can ever know. Once you experience the True Presence of God, nothing else will ever satisfy.

www.ingramcontent.com/pod-product-compliance
Lightning Source LLC
Chambersburg PA
CBHW061201070526
44579CB00009B/89